This book is dedicated to my grandchildren and all who want to witness a survivor's testimony.
-C.K.

Acknowledgments

I could not have written this book alone. The first time I spoke about my Holocaust experience in Dr. Bob Liftig's ninth grade Honors English class, he attended my lecture and saw the impact on the students. He said, "Clara, you have to write all this in a book." He was my mentor and the source of constant encouragement, editing my manuscript and praising my work. I am deeply indebted to him.

The one who typed and corrected my English style, affected by all the languages I speak, was Gia LoScalzo, my former French student who worked tirelessly, never complained about my sentence construction or handwriting, and just urged me to write more. Many times tears blurred her vision and she had to stop. When she was in exams, Jeff Mitchell, another student of mine, took over the typing and was also a meticulous worker who introduced me to the secrets of a computer. My grandson gave me his old laptop that helped me to be more independent in writing. My husband's death made me face my mortality and my mission to tell the world my story.

Wherever the Westchester Holocaust Education Center sent me to speak, the students urged me to write my story so that others may know it. My grandchildren were too young to help me, but their love and future inspired me to tell them my legacy: "Never forget." My son, always concerned for my well-being, worried that I would suffer again as I relived and reconstructed the experiences through writing. My friend Imre Berczeller was always available to help me and support me in my endeavors.

I would also like to thank Paul Jeffries for his artistic creation of the cover; and Andrea Meld for permission to use her poem Witness.

Please read this story for its historical value and understand that my unique memoir of us – my mother and me – is only one of six million that could be told. I am here to speak for myself and for all those who died and cannot speak for themselves.

My greatest support was my mother, who begged me even one week before her death, "Darling, finish your book." That was her last request: to immortalize our Holocaust experiences.

Witness
By Andrea Meld

And we shall be a witness for our times
The grey and the white, the black and the brown;
Far off clouds obscure the hills where ravens fly
The sound of trumpets, drums and thunder
And then—stillness, smoke and ashes

And we shall be a witness for our times
They will ask
Why did no one speak out
Why did no one care
Why didn't anyone do anything
Why was nothing done

And we shall be a witness for our times
Why was it too soon far
Why was it too late
Why were we all paralyzed
Like dreamers in their sheep

And we shall be a witness for our times
Why was it too soon far
Why was it too late
Why were we all paralyzed
Like dreamers in their sleep

And we shall be a witness for our times
Why did we listen to them
Why didn't we listen to others
Why were all our efforts in vain
Why did no one stop
Why did nothing begin
It was not enough
And we shall be a witness for our times

Contents

My parents' wedding

Chapter One:
My Earliest Memories

Dear Rachel and Robert, my dear grandchildren:

1995: It took me fifty years to commit myself to writing the story of our family. You are the first readers of my book. The death of your grandfather, my husband Paul, only increased my compulsion to tell our saga. Only your great-grandmother and I remain of both sides of your father's family as survivors of one of the worst catastrophes of humankind. We can still relate to you the truth, the real history, and the unbelievable events of this century. I will try to be a voice for your forty-four relatives who are silent forever and can never testify.

Pepi, my mother and your great-grandmother, is in her hundredth year and helps a great deal in reminding me of past happenings. She is the oldest Holocaust survivor in the United States and has vivid memories of many details that I remember only vaguely from my childhood. To me, no matter how old I get, she will always be "Mama."

You may reach a point in your lives when you will ask questions about your father's family and you will want to know why he is the only related Knopfler left, maybe anywhere. Today I will begin our saga and I promise that I will tell you the story up until your father, grandfather, and I arrived in the United States in 1962. From that point on, your Dad can tell you the story, because he was seven years old when the SS America, a beautiful ship, brought us to New York from Le Havre, France.

My early childhood was happy, but not so easy. I was the second child of two, and a girl. My name in Hungarian was "Klari" which became "Clara" when I was married and lived in Roumania and later, in the United States. My brother Zoli, the first born, was the only one who carried the family name "Deutsch," so he was considered "special." My father was the oldest of four brothers, and even after nineteen years, none of them had had a boy. Morris, his brother who lived in New York, had no children at all. Harry had one daughter, and my uncle, Gyula, in Romania had five. Each time he expected a boy, but each time instead, a beautiful girl was born. After five tries he and his wife gave up. My father had five sisters. Maybe I was a little jealous of my brother who, of sixteen grandchildren, was the only heir to the family name.

My memories of childhood go back to when I was four years old and perhaps even a little earlier. We lived in the little village of Cehul-Silvaniei, Transylvania, in

Northern Romania. I remember walking to nursery school alone at first until I knocked on the door of my closest friend, Hedi. I stopped briefly to watch her eat her copious breakfast, mine was simpler and faster, and then we walked hand in hand to the home of a third little girl, Nusi. She was already waiting for us on her porch. We headed for the nursery school that was five hundred yards away, but it seemed much longer. I remember wondering would I ever be as smart as Hedi and her sisters, Lucu and Iren? And would I ever be as obnoxious as those boys who teased and made fun of us? Someday, I thought, I would tell them how nasty they were.

I remember noticing how much attention Hedi and her sisters got from their parents and how elaborate their cooking was. They had a cook who baked fresh bread, cakes, and cookies every day. They always had a big basket of muffins on the table -- thirty or forty of them -- and in no time they were eaten. I loved those muffins but I took only one or two at the most. I would have been ashamed to have eaten more. I don't think I envied them for their big house and cook, though. I always thought our house, with many more books and pictures, was homier.

I also have the vivid picture of the small grocery store on our way; the smell of the various spices of Mr. Goldfarb's little shop tempted us on early spring days when his door was open. Handmade soaps were in the window; coffee beans were roasting in the pancake pans over the oven that was hidden behind the drape between their store and kitchen. Hedi and I had to go down four or five steps from the sidewalk to enter their store. Little bells hung from the top of the door and they would ring when we reached the bottom of the stairs. The smell of yeast and fresh rolls mingled, and we could hardly wait until Mr. Goldfarb gave us a roll, some freshly made butter, and one green pepper to eat for lunch. We tried to have only a bite from this in the morning so we could save it until noon. If we behaved and waited patiently until the other customers were served, he added one hard candy wrapped in colored paper.

I remember my first day in kindergarten. Hedi didn't want to stay and she cried her head off; she wanted to go home. She was given wooden blocks, lots of toys, and all the attention, but still was inconsolable. I had found the kids very friendly and I got busy with them right away. My mother always had to help my father in his store, and my brother Zoltán was often sick at home, so she felt that I would have to learn to cope with my little world on my own.

Zoltán had to have more attention; he had been almost blind since his childhood. My Grandmother Luisa had noticed five weeks after his birth that Zoltán's eyes did not focus. After a few months, my parents took him to an eye doctor who told them that both his eyes were weak, especially the right one. It was probably the fault of the midwife who had pushed his head too strenuously, he said. You can imagine how concerned my parents were. The doctor also told them not to do anything about this until my brother was stronger and at least seven years old, but my parents worried that this would be too late. They searched for a doctor who could restore his eyesight. Meanwhile, he needed special attention. He was very intelligent, much more than I. He began playing the violin at the age of six and began piano lessons at seven. We got along though, and practically never fought because I always gave in.

My mother was very attached to Zoltán and was always tending to his needs. He hoped to become a concert pianist. These days went fast. We were busy and I loved my kindergarten teacher, Doamna Maria, who had white hair and many wrinkles around her eyes. She smiled a lot, but her orders were firm. She spoke Romanian to us; at home we spoke Hungarian, but we understood her clear voice and she used her hands a great deal when explaining the games we played.

In kindergarten there were a few children who were not toilet trained; I could never be in this situation. My mother told me later that at one year old my brother and I were toilet trained. We had a white tin pot shaped like a hat with two handles, and one other that we kept under our bed in case we needed it at night or in the early morning. I remember one morning I decided to amuse my brother after having filled the pot. Zoltán laughed so hard that my mother came in from the kitchen and was speechless at the incredible sight. My head was completely covered while here and there brown stuff curled near my ears. Then my mother laughed too, telling us that according to Romanian superstition this would bring good luck in the future.

You see, Robert and Rachel, I always considered myself lucky.

I got more attention from my father, although he spent lots of time with his shoe business. At night he played with me, told me stories, and walked with me in the little streets of our village. Sometimes he took both Zoltán and me, and we walked on the paved sidewalk in front of the middle school on the rich side of town. We passed the courthouse and the houses of the lawyer, doctor, and priest. The sidewalk was paved with small tiles resembling those in the bathrooms in New York and L.A. and it ran about two hundred yards in front of the houses, was very wide (twenty yards or more), and was about twenty steps below people's front doors. On the other side there were at least fifteen acacia that bloomed in spring; their scent was so beautiful that it still lives in my memory so when I think of it, I can smell them again.

We often took the flowers and munched on them as they were full of honey. There were a few chamomile trees whose leaves we dried and we drank the tea when we had upset stomachs and also used it for washing our faces to help beautify our skin. We called this walkway "sima jarda" (smooth sidewalk) and we lived so near to it we thought of it as our own. Zoltán's piano teacher lived at the very end of the street and on the other side of the steps was our synagogue, the center of our religious, cultural, and social lives.

My father used to hold our hands as we walked, and we sang in rhythm, "sétálunk sétálunk egy kis dombon lecsücsülünk, csücs (Let's walk, let's walk, and let's crouch on a little hill, crouch)!" We would take five steps and he would say, "Now kiss each other," while twirling us to catch each of us in front of him. We would laugh at this sudden change of pace, and it was fun.

Later, at the age of twelve, I would feel the romance of this place, but while as still little as I was, asked my father why the people kissed and embraced for so long. There were benches under the trees and young lovers were holding hands or embracing in the semi-darkness or in the moonlight surrounded by darkness and the mystic sounds of birds, crickets, frogs, all croaking for love. My father would say, "Oh, they are saying good-bye to each other. They don't know when they will meet again." And his warm brown eyes would smile at me.

Chapter Two: Reflections: Our Family

My Uncle Gyula had a textile and tailor shop next to our shoe store. He was very successful in his business and in his social life. He married the cantor's daughter and this added to his prestige in the community. Together they had five daughters; each time they expected a son. They stopped trying to have a son after Tirza, their fifth daughter. Uncle Gyula was so proud of his beautiful girls. My grandparents had five sons and six daughters and only my Dad had a son, Zoltán, to carry the family name. Uncle Gyula and my father were very good friends and shared with each other all family problems. They thought of the well-being of each family member. They helped their widowed mother raise their nine siblings, marry off the girls, and support the family. Two of their siblings died: Ilona, the older girl, died of scarlet fever after World War I, and Ignatz, the oldest boy who never married and would have been responsible for supporting his mother, died of appendicitis. My father and Gyula then shared the responsibility for their mother.

In 1922, two of their sisters, Margaret and Rose, seventeen and eighteen years old respectively, were married and emigrated to the United States with the help of an aunt who sent them affidavits. Soon after, Morris, who was also married, followed his sisters to New York. Finally in 1929, Harry, the youngest brother, left Romania. The boys had found a better life and escaped having to join the Romanian army.

These American children worked very hard in the new country. They had very little education (six years in elementary classes at the maximum), no special skills, and no knowledge of English. They struggled for their existence. Fortunately, the two girls knew some sewing and became seamstresses while their husbands were tailors. Uncle Morris worked in a hardware store with his wife, Scheindy, by his side. When Harry arrived in America alone, he tried unsuccessfully to learn to sew. He then worked with Morris in the hardware business. After a couple of years, they began a partnership and opened their own hardware store. Margaret's little home became the center of the American family. There each member found his shelter.

It did not take long for each of them to begin sending money monthly to their mother so she could support the youngest children, particularly the girls, Berta and Emma. (Their other sister, Ida, had married). My father helped the whole family with shoes and essentials, such as flour and sugar. Gyula kept his mother in his home until all the children who could help, especially the Americans, did so, and then had a small house built for her in his backyard.

Grandma Luisa loved this home and kept it so clean that I tiptoed through the rooms so as not to dirty the floors. (I did this even although all the grandchildren were required to take their shoes off before entering). Luisa brought up eleven children without help, and they all learned her neatness without rebelling against her meticulous character. Each of them had a responsibility that they carried out without questioning. Emulating their hardworking mother, the older children took care of the younger ones. But my grandmother never smiled. She had lost her husband and two grown children, and never recovered from her mourning sadness.

She had us in her house after synagogue every Saturday afternoon for cocoa and cake, her specialty, but the forced discipline in her home spoiled the pleasure of visiting. All her life she wore a black scarf. She was always cold and bitter. My father's respect for his mother was perhaps deeper than his love for her. As a child I sensed this and held it against her. I loved my mother and did not understand my grandmother's coldness toward her daughters and sons-in-law in Romania. Even so, she spoke highly of her children in America, remarking often on their generosity. And she fulfilled her duty toward her family, feeling a strong responsibility for their health, careers, and religious beliefs, but I never saw her kiss or hug any of her children.

Her grandchildren (all of us) were supposed to kiss her hand when leaving her house, but she seldom kissed us back. She rarely came to our house and almost never told us stories, except about her own family, who were singers and very educated. I still have a great uncle, Pali Purjesz (now Pálfai) who lives in Budapest. He wrote a mathematics book for colleges and was the Dean of the Polytechnic University in Budapest. His cousins were opera singers and survived by hiding in Budapest but they died in poverty in 1948. My grandmother spoke to us about these nephews and nieces and about what education means to a person. Unfortunately, her children did not have professions, because their father had died and she could not afford high school or college for them.

My father was more self-educated than the others, especially in music and literature. He married a pretty girl, my mother, but she also lacked a formal education. I thoroughly resented my grandmother's attitude because she objected to my ambition. Unlike her other grandchildren, I wanted to go to a different city and study. Later, Emma's son Misu, who was two years younger than I, studied with me in the same Jewish school. My grandmother respected his ambition because he was a boy. Misu and his parents died in Auschwitz.

My mother's family, the Becks, was different. Although they lived in the same country and practiced the same religion as my father's family, their lives and values were geared towards intellectual advancement. My grandfather, Martin Beck, became a widower at forty. His second wife, my grandmother Regina Hirsch, was twenty years his junior. She was beautiful, skillful, and an excellent housewife. She looked up to her handsome husband who was a landowner educated in Jewish studies. She was impressed with his generosity toward his poorer relatives who always needed his help. She recognized in him the same values that her family had instilled in her.

Martin and Regina's first child died, but they later had five children: first two sons, then my mother, and then another two sons. My mother hardly remembers her father's family. Her grandfather died before she was born, but she was told stories about him. It is said that he was educated in the best Yeshiva of the country, at Pozsony, and was unhappy when his father could not support him any longer in school as a result of a bad flood and the subsequent bad crop. He had to get married to bring to his family a dowry that could be invested in the land. Luckily, although the marriage was arranged, they genuinely liked one another. Even so, he was not a good businessman, and they were poor. One day he went to the market with a one-horse coach to buy a cow or goat to provide milk for his family. He could not find one that he could afford, so he set off for home frustrated. On the road in front of him, an elegant two horse coach had stopped at the village fountain to quench the horses' thirst. My mother's grandfather slowed down about three hundred yards away from the fountain, waiting humbly, and not wanting to interrupt the drinking horses.

He held himself back, especially because he saw the owner of the horses descending from the coach and recognized him as the richest landlord in the region. The man pulled his pipe from his jacket, and with it, a small bag accidentally dropped. The driver finished feeding his horses and hurried to continue the trip because night was approaching.

My great-grandfather tried to yell that the landlord had dropped something, but no one heard him. When he reached the fountain, he picked up the bag and saw that it was filled with money. The owner was too far away for my great-grandfather to catch up to, and when he got home it was too late for him to do anything. The next day he told his wife that he must go to the village where this rich landlord lived and return the bag. The landlord's little castle was closed to him, however, as the butler did not want to let him in. But my great-grandfather persisted and told the butler that he had to see the landlord because he had something important to give to him. Finally, the landlord, curious about a stubborn Jew, agreed to admit him. When he saw the bag with all the coins in it, he wanted to reward the honest man who had returned it. He gave my great-grandfather twelve gallons of pure alcohol as compensation. My great-grandfather made thousands of drinks out of it, and became a rich man.

My maternal grandfather was educated and had a comfortable life. I spent one vacation that I remember vividly at my grandparents' house. I was six years old and very curious and my grandmother was sweet and permissive. I could walk in her orchard that was full of fruits of varying ripeness and eat them instead of lunch. I could climb the trees with the other farmers' children who also played in our orchard. They came home with me and we chatted in our kitchen.

Baby chickens covered with yellow down and their mother hen always surrounded my grandmother and she was constantly feeding them with all kinds of grains. I would disappear and climb a ladder up to a stable that held no animals, only hay, straw, and a lot of junk that I explored, never managing to see it all. There were old pictures, tools, big old-fashioned clothes, children's toys, and many old books. I would spend hours in this attic, but one afternoon I fell asleep and it was dark when I awoke.

I hurried to step down the ladder, but the garden worker, not realizing that someone was sleeping above, had removed it. I fell fifteen feet to the hard ground and broke my upper arm bone completely. I screamed until someone came to pick me up, and then I fainted. I don't remember how I got to the main house or how my mother was notified, only that I was taken to the nearest hospital screaming as if someone were killing me for the entire two hours it took to get there. A doctor put my arm in a cast, but did it the wrong way. My parents took me to another hospital in Zilah where the surgeon had to break the bone and place it in a new cast. I could not play for six precious weeks. This was my last vacation before attending first grade.

Rachel and Robert

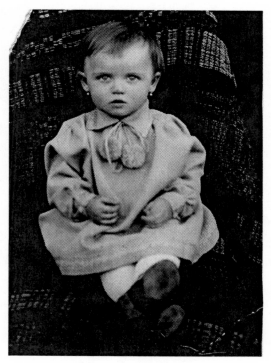

Clara 3 years old

My father in W.W.I

Chapter Three: School Days

Rachel and Robert, you are both not yet in middle school, and you are at the age when it is so important to trust your teacher and yourself so that you can build a strong foundation of knowledge underneath your future house of accomplishments. My four elementary classes were the basis of my positive attitude toward both school and study, and may be the reason I spent forty years as a teacher. In Hungary, we had twenty to twenty-five students in our class with the same teacher who began teaching us in first grade and continued with us until we graduated from fourth. She was Romanian born and very proud of her nationality. If someone called her by her Hungarian first name, she corrected him clearly. I did not know then how much animosity there was between the Hungarian and Romanian people, even though they shared the same village and socio-economic situations, but not the same language or religion.

I loved my teacher Dna. Simon Vasiliu; she was strict, but understanding. She built up our self confidence from the very first day of the school year. I thought she could never be wrong; she was always fair and she only asked what we were able to know. Her family lived across the street from us in a house much nicer than the one in which we lived. Her husband was a lawyer, they had three adorable daughters, and they were brought up in exemplary joyfulness.

At the end of fourth grade I was first in my class. Papusa was the middle school principal's daughter, a Romanian non-Jew. She ranked second and was very bright. The boy Joe who ranked third was an underachiever who preferred to play rather than study. I was awarded both the gold medal engraved with the Romanian king's portrait Carol, and a signed picture of his thirteen year old son Mihai (he is still alive today and living in Switzerland). I was also given a certificate and a beautiful anthology of short stories. My parents were very proud of me, and for a while I was the happiest girl in the village.

My brother Zoltán continued his elementary and middle school education in Budapest in a special school, and when he came home and learned of my achievement he said he would not make fun of my piano playing anymore because I had earned his respect by excelling in other areas of learning, although he was still very condescending about my accordion playing. I had chosen the accordion as my musical instrument. I lacked confidence in my ability to play the piano, because Zoltán was my brother and playing the piano was his life. When I returned from the concentration camps I tried to learn more piano and accordion, but my heart was no longer in it because of what had happened to Zoltán and me in the camps. I loved and still love music, but will never play any instrument again. Music, however, can be a great friend in joy and sadness.

I finished four elementary classes, but could not continue as there was no middle school in my village. There was only a commercial school, which had no connection to academic work, and offered only two or perhaps four additional classes where one could earn a certificate as a plumber, hairdresser, mechanic, tailor's apprentice, or dressmaker. This would not satisfy my father's expectations for me, so my parents decided to get a tutor for my friends and me to be taught four hours daily. We could take exams in a neighboring town's public school.

Our tutor was a well-educated teacher, Madame Galusca, who taught in the commercial school, but she was a slave driver. She would pump into us one subject after the other: Math, Social Studies, and Geography. She was only relaxed when she taught us poetry and she was the first person to make us study art for art's sake. She read us descriptions of nature in rhymes — the changing colors of autumn leaves, the loving flight of butterflies — all in a soft voice that was neither monotonous nor singing.

She was a science teacher, too! What contrasts in her personality! She was happy with us, her three private students, not only for the extra money but also for the chance we gave her to teach poetry and literature. In fifth grade she taught us Homer, the blind Greek poet, nursery rhymes by Scandinavian poets, and La Fontaine fables translated into Romanian. We had fun. Well, Hedi and I enjoyed it, but Nusi made faces and fell asleep.

In 1939 and 1940 war started in some parts of Europe, but it affected us very little. There were discussions in our house; my uncles told us news about the war of Hitler and the anti-Semitic actions of the Iron Guard. The grownups looked worried and insecure about the future. They listened to the radio and tried to understand the reactions of our government. In the summer of 1940, for example, the Hungarians occupied the northern half of Transylvania, coming back to their sweet land which they had lost after World War I. Because the Hungarians became his allies in the war, Hitler sanctified their return. There was no opposition -- the Romanians could not confront the Third Reich. There were even Jews who welcomed the incoming Hungarian army, but who knew very little about its commitment to Nazi Germany for the price of recapturing Transylvania.

One Friday evening my father returned from the synagogue and told my mother about a man who had escaped from Poland and told outrageous stories about the Nazi regime's atrocities in his country. Jews were the target of their torture. Fortunes, jobs, and houses were taken, synagogues were burnt, and groups of men were taken away — he did not know where. My father thought these were incredible stories and that we did not need to worry.

The Romanians also did these kinds of things, though not in our village. The Iron Guard were the murderers. The Romanian peasants did not go along with the Iron Guards. Their life was so simple and they were contented with very little, living isolated in small villages in the mountains and in straw-covered, thatched houses in the rich valleys two centuries behind western civilization.

My parents wanted to believe that the change might help us but the Romanian Nationalist Party was persecuting Jews. Yet the members of our congregation did not want to listen to the outcry of a Polish stranger who was living for a week or so in different Jewish houses so the authorities could not find him. He pleaded with the Jews to believe him about how the Nazi menace was threatening their seemingly peaceful lives. He urged us to unify and develop some kind of resistance, or to escape our country as soon as we could, perhaps to Eretz-Israel -- Palestine. But the Jews of our village could not think about leaving their little shtetl. Wars come and go, they said. Anti-Semitism always was and always will be. If we are good, working, studying, praying people, God will help us and our families stay together. And Hitler will fail.

The stranger left with tears in his eyes. He could not convince the Jewish population of the danger that would soon shake our whole world. But we children could now see our parents' constant worry. Our future was foggy and insecure they knew; my father's business slowed and anti-Semitic feeling was growing like poisonous mushrooms in the forest. My parents soon lived in a constant fear that we sensed each day. They spent less and less time with us. They spoke Yiddish to each other, so we would not understand. We chose to misunderstand this; we would rather believe that they were ignoring us than that they were concerned about whether we would all live through the coming year.

We were used to being involved in every segment of our family's life: business, entertainment, reading, singing, walking together, shopping, preparing meals and decorating our house for religious holidays such as Purim, Passover, and Sukkoth. These were our great expectations. We were also used to excursions with friends in mountains, rivers, and neighboring forests, but after 1939, all these were impossible to enjoy freely. Even my dear father's optimism, which kept our hopes alive all of these years, was failing. And there was not a sign of relief; things were only getting worse.

In the summer of 1940, the Iron Guard initiated pogroms against Jews and we were very frightened. Then the Hungarians occupied Cehul-Silvaniei with a great parade. Soldiers marched and cavalry rode through the center of our little village. Hungarian women greeted their army in velvet vests and colorful scarves — traditional folk dress. The men wore white cotton culottes with large leather belts, elaborate silver attachments, and either black felt or straw hats. Our maid dressed me up also, but my parents were skeptical about the celebration and about the new administration.

One of the first laws the Hungarians announced was that there would be no public school for Jewish children. In big cities up to two percent of a class could be made up of Jewish students, but not in our tiny village. The same was true for privately tutored students. Other anti-Jewish laws were enacted daily restricting Jewish activities. Only Hungarian education would be allowed now and I had no hope of continuing my seventh grade in our tiny village so I studied Hungarian spelling, reading, and history the whole summer just in case I could take an entrance examination in September to some school for which I might qualify as one of the lucky two percent. Every day I copied pages of stories, memorized poems and the Hungarian history that Hungarian schools taught in the homeland, but it was hopeless — not because I couldn't pass the examination, which I took in September, but because by then no school would accept any of us — not even two percent. Only a miracle could now save the Jewish childrens' educational upbringing.

My house

264. *Szilágycsehi.* Orthodox synagogue. — *Orthodox zsinagóga.* — .סילאג׳יצ׳הי, אורת

The Synagogue in my village

Chapter Four: Transitions

My childhood changed suddenly; there would be no normal transition from child to teenager. I had many friends and was a popular girl, especially in my elementary classes. When I was tutored in fifth and sixth grade, still under Romanian regime, we were together mostly with the group of children we met daily. The others, mainly those children whose parents could afford it, were sent to boarding schools in different cities, or to private schools in towns where they had relatives with whom they could live. We met with these friends only on winter and spring vacations.

My boyfriends, Gabi and Peter, wrote me letters full of poetry that said they missed me. They counted the days and hours until they could come home just to hold hands and share our joy or sadness. Dear Rachel and Robert, I must tell you that sometimes, on rare occasions, the bolder boys would steal kisses in the flower gardens, under the trees, in the vineyard, but it was so innocent and sweet.

Then the Hungarian army came. The officers needed rooms in private houses as they would not sleep among the soldiers in the tents. We had two bedrooms and an entrance with a long hall between them. This is where I slept when my brother Zoli was home on vacations. That summer, however, I had to sleep in my parents' room and my brother slept in the hall. He noticed that "our officer," who occupied our second bedroom, a twenty-something blond and handsome young man, would come into the entrance hall whenever he came home and peek into my parents' room, although the glass was opaque.

He would ask Zoli, "Is your pretty sister still reading, or has she fallen asleep?"

Zoli was very private and jealous so he would answer, "I don't know and I won't find out."

During the week I hardly saw the officer, but on Sundays it was impossible to avoid his presence or his orderly constant demands for hot water, fresh linen, and towels as he treated our house as if it were a hotel and he a high-paying occupant. I was in the kitchen, but very curious to see the good looking officer in his close-fitted uniform with glittering buttons. He only came in when his orderly had gotten him all that was necessary for his getting dressed up to go to the village church.

I admired him. He impressed me in spite of my father's warnings to beware of army men because they are not stable "friends" -- here one day and gone to another town the next. My cheeks burned whenever I saw him; I would smile at him and he would compliment me. He even checked my spelling in Hungarian, and was surprised when I told him that for six years I had learned my subjects in Romanian only. All of this happened in front of Mama or Dad or my brother. I was never left alone with him for a moment I did not know why -- I was only thirteen.

But Dad was right about soldiers. One day the officer came to say good-bye without prior announcement. One evening in late summer he came to my parents' room, thanked them for our kind acceptance of a Hungarian soldier, and for giving up my bedroom to a stranger. He shook hands with my father and brother, elegantly kissed my mother's hand, and then, very embarrassed, came to me, turned his back to my parents, covered my face with small kisses, and finally, quickly kissed my lips. It was so fast and so unexpected that I could not utter a word. He said quietly that he would never forget me, and then left without looking back. Mama said that he had tears in his eyes. That was my first real kiss and I have never forgotten it.

I reflected on that scene many times. I would not tell about it to my friends -- it was a "stupid, unimportant thing" in those times. My rational Mama saw me day-dreaming and, with her ever-present common sense, talked to me on a late August afternoon when no one was around. She spoke about the events that a little girl goes through from childhood to a young womanhood, many of which are often unnoticed by others. These, she said, were nice to remember, but should not be dwelt upon. There was a lot for me to look forward to many new things. A whole world would separate me from this young man, and futures are unpredictable. Mama had found a school for me to attend where I could finish my education. I should concentrate on my new school year, she said, and on new friends.

Mama told me about the new school that was founded with great difficulty. It was a school for Jewish children who were not accepted to any school in Transylvania. Jewish administrators with outstanding merits from the Hungarian government would run the school. These included Antal Mark, a famous mathematician, and Dr. Moshe Weinberger (now Carmilly), an erudite rabbi from Kolozsvar. They had been expelled from the universities and public schools because they were Jewish; but they were the best teachers in the country who had accepted small salaries just to survive and have the chance to teach.

Their standards were high, as was their level of preparation. No teacher held less than a master's degree; the majority held doctorates in teaching. Our curriculum was richer than any public school in Hungary and the high authorities of the State Board of Education administered the requirements for accreditation. The twelfth grade had a final examination (the baccalaureate) which had to be taken in front of a panel of twelve Hungarian teachers of every subject. They could ask any question they chose from the material covered in fifth through twelfth grade. In order to set an example, we were told; we had to be better, more hardworking, and more disciplined than any public school student. The school offered six languages (Hungarian, German, Latin, French, Hebrew, and English), six years of math, six years of science, eight years of social studies, art, music, crafts, shorthand, home economics, gym, extracurricular activities, and afternoon classes. There were clubs for philosophy, sociology, electives, and sports. Some of us were in school from eight o'clock until one in the afternoon, when we would go home for lunch. After lunch we returned to school until five o'clock. We participated in plays, concerts, and listening to music, and every Saturday we were present in synagogue where some of us sang in the chorus.

We knew that the school's survival depended on us. The quality of work we did and our results would be compared with the regular schools from which we were segregated. There was no other way for us to exist than by excelling. Even so, we felt very isolated, looked down upon, and stigmatized by the other schools.

This was not easy to accept, we were just children very much like the others. We studied, smiled, and loved. There was no reasonable explanation. More and more we heard that we were regarded negatively because we were Jews, and this hit us hard, especially when we began to see changes taking place every week in our little community and in our own families.

But I never felt happier in any school or university than I did in this Jewish school. We all felt safe, together, cared for, encouraged, helped, and treated with dignity by every teacher. The administrators never pushed for more money from our parents -- they knew that the parents contributed the maximum they could afford for their children's education.

We, the students of the new school, wholeheartedly cooperated with its goal. We learned and taught those who needed our help. I tutored a fourth grader, and when I received a little pocket money in payment around Hanukkah, I bought a necktie for my father as a birthday gift. He wore it with so much pride.

The school's philosophy was "Non scholae sed vitae discimus" ("We study for life -- not for school") and our parents felt that the best investment they could make, and maybe the only one, was an investment in their children's education. As my father used to say, "Anything that is in your mind cannot be taken away."

How right he was. The Hungarians took our house with everything my parents had earned by their hard work. They took our store, our books, our schools, and our liberty, but if we could survive this ordeal, our education would remain part of us.

My parents had two children in two different towns and two different schools. My brother was in Budapest studying piano and living in a boarding school for talented students. He came home only once a year for the long summer vacation because, under the Romanian government, traveling was made difficult because of the expense and complications of having to issue a Romanian passport to a young boy.

I lived in my mother's cousin's house. My Aunt Ester lived in Kolozsvar in a second marriage to a tailor who gambled and did not contribute to her household. Ester had a son who was a doctor who helped her somewhat and, while I lived with her, my father helped by regularly sending packages of flour, eggs, honey, butter, and even live poultry which were more readily available from the peasant farmers of small villages than from the shops in towns. Aunt Ester was grateful and my parents knew that I would be safe and taken care of with their relatives.

The only thing I did not like was the filth that my uncle's cigar and cigarette smoking created on the walls. One night when my aunt and her husband went to sleep early, I washed all the walls and the ceiling and windows with cold water and soap, and went to sleep at seven in the morning pretending to have been in bed all night. When my aunt woke up and saw the room, she was amazed and thanked me with tears in her eyes. She said she knew I was a good hearted little girl, but she had not imagined that I would ever spend the whole night cleaning and washing the house to make her happy.

My aunt was very sick, however. She suffered from a rare liver disease for more than two years and it killed her two months before the school year ended. Aunt Ester was the first person I ever saw in physical agony, having to struggle every minute for her life until she finally died. I remember her son sobbing at her bedside without noticing my presence.

He cried out, "Mama, you helped me, sent me to Padua to study when I could not get into medical school here in Romania. You worked day and night so that I could become a physician, and now I cannot save your life! Mama, forgive me, please. I love you."

He said this while kissing her hands and face and stroking her hair until her breathing ceased completely. Then he put his fingers on her eyelids, hugged her once more, and turned around and saw me. He told me the nicest thing: that with my youthful laughter I had brought joy to my aunt during the last two years of her life, and that she was so happy to have had me in her house.

I was shocked at facing the mortality of a human being for the first time, and shocked at Uncle Miki's suffering. I wondered how this narrow line between life and death was possible, and was overwhelmed by the pain of the survivors. But I remembered reading somewhere that our loved ones die only if we forget them, and that if we remember their faces, deeds, and words, they will always live in our hearts.

My class in 1942. I am located in the 2nd row the top, 8th face from the left.

Chapter Five:
Love and Thunder

The sudden death of Aunt Ester left me without a home. I needed a place to live for the remaining six weeks of the school year, from May to June. Oli Rossler, one of my classmates, offered me a bed in a one-bedroom apartment she shared with her father. Her mother had died when Oli was ten years old. Her father was a music teacher with no steady income who was not able to get a job in the Jewish school; they struggled every day for survival.

I have never seen such poverty. Their apartment floor was uncarpeted concrete. Oli and I slept in the bedroom and her father slept on a sofa in the living room. Posters of famous musicians covered the walls. On the dressing table were medals and trophies that Oli's mother and father had won in concerts. Oli's mother had been a singer. My parents never saw Oli's apartment and never heard me complain about it because I did not want to add to their other worries.

In spite of this misery, Oli had an incredible optimism that she projected with a beautiful face and teeth, sparkling blue eyes, and thick blond hair sometimes braided in a crown around her head. I thought she looked just like a teenaged model. She liked to recite poems with meaningful content; she wasn't interested in "Art for art's sake." We shared a love for literature. I remember a poem she chanted every night like a lullaby. It dealt with a poor family in which the mother comforts her child with the power of faith --the treasure of poor people. She used this as a prayer that gave her hope for better dreams and new mornings. This philosophy in fifty rhyming stanzas was Oli's emotional nourishment.

The problem that preoccupied us now was our immediate future. Every day was full of new edicts against the Jews. In cities, these instructions were posted in the streets and in the post offices where everyone could see them. In my little village, the town crier would be preceded by a drummer who would read the orders of the mayor. One day the village drummer appeared in the center of the main square twenty yards from our house, beating his drum so all could hear. When the people surrounded him, his drumming ceased and he began reading: Jews should not congregate, go to restaurants, or to market before 10 a.m. and they should return home no later than 5 p.m. We began to live in a constant nightmare, worrying and wondering what would happen next.

Young men, sixteen and older who were not in school, were called upon to do field work, i.e., slave labor, without pay and very little food. They slept in tents and their work was supervised by the Hungarian soldiers. The Hungarian army requisitioned the private houses of Jewish families who lived nearby. Older men who had small children or were not in the army because they were Jews also contributed their physical labor to winning Hitler's war. They took my father in 1943 with only an hour's notice. They told him to take shirts and underwear for a week, and food for three days. This was during my spring vacation.

I thought my mother was going to lose her mind. She was crying, shouting, and asking us how could she alone possibly support her family especially as food was scarce at that time. Her uncontrolled spontaneity and panic scared us. I can still see her face distorted with pain and agony.

Luckily, my father's group was sent home after six weeks. They could not do field work -- it was impossible to cultivate the ground because there had been so much rain that the seeds were washed out. You can imagine the shortage of crops and the general panic that ensued. Our little community was in turmoil.

Even the Hungarian population worried about the outcome. The mayor and his administration enforced dictatorial rules and encouraged spying on "thy neighbor" and denouncing him if he were found to be against the rulers, especially if he were a "Jew friend." We had great neighbors; both Jews and non-Jews. But those who were Christians had been warned that if they socialized with us they would be punished. They were told that they should not question why. We could not even meet secretly in this small village even though everyone knew each other. We were afraid of being denounced and we cared about the safety of our Christian friends.

By my freshman year we simply couldn't afford to continue our education in Kolozsvar. I had to be tutored at home, and took the exams in the Jewish school. But for my sophomore year, my father had persuaded my mother to help me become a regular student if we could find a suitable boarding school, and I received a full scholarship from the Jewish school. Then the summer of 1943 came to an end. The next school year looked very gloomy -- my sophomore year. In September, I found out that Oli had become very friendly with my closest friend, Sam Katz. She had written me in the summer and said that she had taken my place and become his girlfriend. I was disappointed in her, but few things seemed important in those days. Besides, I had fallen in love with my friend Blimu's older brother, Ervin, during my freshman year when I was tutored at home. I knew him and had liked him since elementary school, but he was two years older. During middle school and high school he only came home on vacations.

In September my best friend Babuci's parents were to take me in to board in their house. The year 1943 proved difficult for Ervin. He was expelled from school because he belonged to a socialist youth group. He told me, however, that he was on probation and had to go to the police station every day so the police could monitor him to determine whether or not he was involved in any subversive activity. Ervin's parents had paid a good deal of money so that he would be paroled and not jailed like the other members of his group. Ironically, had he been jailed, he would have avoided death in Auschwitz.

Ervin belonged to the richest Jewish family in our village. His parents were produce merchants dealing with wheat, barley, and other grains in huge quantities. But Ervin had joined a clandestine Marxist Communist revolutionary group. Of course, his involvement in the group and his socialist ideas were in contrast to his upbringing.

Later we found out that at least ten youths from our village met regularly in great secrecy to spread communistic ideas according to which all people were equal regardless of race, religion, or sex. They advocated the re-distribution of wealth from the rich to the poor and freedom of speech and of the press. Ervin never told me anything about his secret meetings, but I was very impressed by his readings and knowledge of the economic and cultural differences among the social classes. Every day before he was to appear at the police station, he came to our house and stayed until my parents came home. We knew that we were being watched also.

My parents objected to Ervin's visits, but they also knew how much this friendship meant to both of us at a time when we were isolated from our other friends. My mother also realized how much we cared for each other.

We studied together read, sang, discussed, and finally, we fell in love with each other. Dad, the romantic, gave in first, because he knew that in September I would go back to school and Ervin would miss these afternoons because he had to stay in our village.

Babuci and I were good friends. Luckily, in Babuci's friendship I found a home. We studied together and walked to school together, but we had different friends. She stayed with a religious group of friends while my friends had more freedom and were more liberal. We went to movies, Saturday afternoon dances at youth centers, and we socialized more with boys (though we were supervised because we were only in the eighth grade).

We had literary and musical auditions and organized small groups in which we discussed philosophy and political views in general, but mainly from the point of view of the Jewish problem. We discussed why we were isolated, why we could not have non-Jewish friends, why we could not attend public schools, and how our parents were able to make a living despite the new laws appearing every month that increasingly curtailed our life.

Every day I received a letter from Ervin, and every two weeks he sent me a package of sweets-chocolate, cookies, marzipan, and bonbons. He was able to buy them because he was both rich and generous. We also exchanged books and poems monthly from September until March, when they sent all students home from school because no Jews could have any education anymore. There were more important things for us to do: helping The Germans win the war.

During Christmas vacation that year Ervin talked to me seriously about the times we lived in and the future. He was very skeptical. Still, he hoped that after the war we would get married, and said that no matter what he had to cope with, this hope would help him survive. I was not yet seventeen and he was nineteen. He saw no solution to the Jewish "problem." He had studied the history of the Jews and realized that, although anti-Semitism had existed since the time of the Romans, it had never been so fierce.

My father grew closer to Ervin and they discussed history. Dad's eternal optimism, which he always showed on the surface, consoled us all. He used to say that after the darkness comes the dawn. There must be some solution, Dad thought. After all, families, friends and loved ones were still together.

"We are not criminals," Dad said. "They won't send us to jail." My father felt sorry for our tormented youth, but he said our ordeal would soon be over.

The authorities had confiscated all the radios and the newspapers and were lying in order to hide the truth: that Hitler had been losing the war since 1942. His army had suffered its first great defeat in Stalingrad and never recovered. What we did not know was that Hitler would exterminate almost all of Europe's Jews.

Chapter Six:
Breakdown

At least two months elapsed since I wrote the last chapter. The closer I get to describing the destruction of our family, the harder it becomes to fulfill my mission. In March 1944 Hitler's army invaded Hungary. A week later my brother came home from Budapest, completely devastated by the events that had taken place in the capital. The Hungarians had sold their country to the Nazis. Dome Sztojai, the leader of the new government, was Hitler's puppet and even the semblance of Hungary's independence was lost.

On March 28, 1944 we were all home. All Jewish children and relatives had to return to their families. There were rumors that we would be sent to work outside of our community -- a job that would help the Germans win the war. Mama tried to prepare the Friday night dinner that we loved so much. Dad and Zoltán went to the synagogue, and I set the table with the white tablecloth and lit the room with the four candles that my mother and I blessed. It was so beautiful and so solemn.

Mama had a special prayer that she said with humble eloquence and an intonation that sounded as if she were the only woman who could talk to God. She asked only to be at peace and with her family to stay together. The plates, the silverware, the silver cup for Kiddush wine, the blue napkins, glasses, salt shaker. Everything had to be in its place to enhance the warmth of the family's supper. It was so different from our everyday routine. The kitchen was immaculate, the dining room fireplace was warm and needed because it was a cold March evening, and the aroma of chicken soup filled our house.

Mama put on her holiday dress and covered her hair with a white scarf. I changed my blouse and put on my mother's high-heeled shoes to impress my brother. We waited for the men to come. My father arrived first with a pleasing smile and wished us a good Shabbat. Then my brother followed, singing a Friday night Hebrew song. Father kissed Mama, called her "my pretty wife," and covered my head with his hands and blessed me first and then blessed my brother. He hugged us with his long arms around us and we kissed each other. Then he filled the silver cup with red wine and sang the Kiddush with the warm tenor voice that we loved so much.

We wished that this scene would last forever. We tried to forget everything that surrounded us: the ugly facts, the rumors, and the world's hostility towards Jews. We thought that as long as we were together no evil could touch us. We tasted the wine after our parents and were then ready to say the blessing for the bread. Dad cut the challah and gave a small piece to each of us. Mama brought in the bowl of hot chicken soup (Jews could no longer get geese) and white radishes, and we began our dinner.

We used to have lively conversations on Friday nights. Our weeks had always begun on Sunday, but for three years the mayor had ordered Jews to open stores for business on Saturday, not Sunday. My father and some other merchants tried to resist; even God rested on Saturday, they said. But the Jews had to give in. So we had only Friday nights for us to talk about everything that had taken place during the past week, and about our upcoming plans.

We were afraid to antagonize the mayor, whose name was Krasznai, as he was like Ivan the Terrible. He called in the resistant Jews one by one to "discuss" the matter, but instead had them beaten and humiliated. He made the old men tremble and displayed his sadistic pleasure with the glee of omnipotent laughter. My father was also called in, but for another reason. The mayor wanted a pair of hunting boots that only my father could make. He had to work alone because he was no longer allowed to have workers. The mayor promised that our store would be closed on Saturdays; however he did not keep his word.

On Saturdays, Mama would sit in the store so my father could go to the synagogue. He never stopped hoping and believing that God would help and that the situation was His test of how faithful and obedient His chosen people could be. We children watched as our parents struggled to face reality and still underplayed their worry in front of us.

April 1, 1944 was The Day of Fools, except for us. It was the day we learned that we would have to wear a yellow star -- a cloth that said "Zsido" (Jew). My mother had to sew it on our coats, jackets, and other clothes. On April 6th, we put them on. It was horrible. I felt like a leper who knows that he does not belong to this society and whose existence is harmful to friends or acquaintances, even if he only greets them from a distance.

My brother stopped going out after 6 p.m., and we were not allowed to be out until 10 a.m. to go to the market at which time there was nothing to left to buy because the fresh vegetables, milk and dairy were already sold. We had no telephone and no radio. We were cut off from the world. Some courageous former customers stepped into the store where my Mama and Dad worked with their one employee, Feri Goldberger, who had come from Romania two years previously as an apprentice. He would have to remain now in Hungary. His brothers Mike and Les were also taught shoe designing by my father, and they lived in our house for three years while my brother and I were in school. They were like family to us. Feri, the youngest brother, was in love with me and said that he would marry me after the war. He knew that I had a boyfriend who was intellectually superior to him, and yet he dreamed of marrying me, working with my father, and belonging to our family. I found out later that he had helped my father hide goods in a box to be saved for my dowry: damask for bedding, a gold bracelet, and some silverware. He also helped my uncle, who had five daughters, dig a big trench for storing goods and clothing, so that when we returned from wherever we were going to be taken, we would at least have something good to wear. By the time I came home one year later, in April, 1945, they were rotten. Feri found the place where the goods were buried and blamed himself for not better insulating the box. But by then I did not care about the loss, because I had lost so much more.

Still, I am nostalgic when I think of how hard my family worked to create a comfortable future for us; how they hoped to make our lives less difficult than theirs. My father had saved five hundred dollars for each of us years before the Holocaust, during the Romanian regime when anti-Semitism hindered our education, but not yet our business. When Mama and I returned, we searched for the money. Mama knew it was buried in the garden somewhere in a pharmaceutical jar, but for weeks we could not find it. Then Mr. Rakosi, a neighbor, helped us locate it, measuring the steps that my mother remembered. He found it and dug it out -- a life saver.

Chapter Seven:
The Village Nightmare

Wearing the yellow star was like carrying our whole body and soul. I always felt the weight on my shoulders, chest, and legs. Even in the time when we were allowed to walk on the streets, I tried to close my eyes or look down so no one could see what I was thinking. My hope was that they might not notice my "Ostrich politics."

Many of my Christian friends with whom I had gone to elementary school were away at a high school in a bigger city, so they did not know about my suffering or what was happening to the Jews of their village. The Easter vacation was at the end of April and they came home. I loved the idea of seeing them, but I was ashamed to tell them about our situation. We could not meet them anyway, and they would have to avoid us. We could not play tennis, basketball, or ping-pong with them. We could not walk with them. Jews were to be forever isolated from human interaction. April was the last month of rumors; soon they became reality. One of the rumors was that our entire families would be taken away from home to an agricultural camp called "Kenyérmezo" (Field of Bread). We would work in the fields during the harvest period, collect the crops, work in mills, and send food as soon as possible to the soldiers who were fighting on the Eastern Front, and everywhere else where Hitler hoped to occupy more territories. After the end of the battle of Stalingrad in 1943, no one believed that he would win, but his orders stood.

There was no indication of what we could take with us. All our valuables already had been confiscated by the Hungarian authorities. We had been given no receipts for what they took: gold, silver, foreign money, stocks, bonds, insurance papers, and foreign investments. Everyone's life savings were taken away without an explanation except one: "Jew." We teenagers could not cope with this answer. Our parents knew that Jews had been persecuted for two thousand years, but this was different.

Friday night in the synagogue was marked more by consternation, perplexity, and fear of what lay ahead, than by prayer. My brother told me that the men formed small groups and discussed the rumors of the week. They heard about other villages or towns where the Jews were already in ghettos. Quarters were emptied, mostly in the poor Jewish sections, and Jews from all parts of the town were transported to this ghetto -- two or three families in a room with one bathroom, or none at all. They cooked in small kitchens and tried to organize their chores in a disciplined way. They did not know how long they would stay there.

We did not know anything specific about our departure: not where, when, or what our new lifestyle would be, so every day was a present for us. We were together and we tried to be gentle with each other. In order not to feel the hopelessness of our situation, we prepared for Passover as we had always done. First, we cleaned the house until it was spotless. Then my father put the last small breadcrumbs in the corner of the kitchen, and along with the dishes sold them symbolically to a Christian friend with the option that after eight days we might buy them back. We brought down from the attic the special set of china and dishes kept solely for use during our holiday. Food always tasted so much better from these dishes. The taste of matzo soaked in fresh coffee, milk, and sugar was so different and delicious, that even now it brings back memories of my short childhood so ruthlessly interrupted by the Holocaust.

The matzo was handmade in our village by the religious housewives who were supervised by the temple's meshgiach, or shames, who himself was authorized for this very important job. Round thick matzos smelling like well-toasted bread were packed individually in clean towels. They were then taken by each family; carefully carrying their precious weight. Everyone had much less than they had the previous year, but we were happy to have anything at all.

We ate potatoes so the dinner would be complete. There was much less meat, wine, and butter, and fewer eggs, but we managed to celebrate as always.

That year we disregarded the material shortage of our feast. The white robe "Kittle," in which my father was to be buried according to Jewish custom, was freshly starched and pressed. The pillow under his right arm showed his authority, pater familias, and no one could see how humiliated he felt by the outside world -- the one that tried to take away his dignity as the provider of his family and the guide to the security of his children.

Father sang the whole story of our Exodus from Egypt. He sang of our people wandering through the desert, of God's punishment of the wicked pharaoh, and of our settlement in the new land of the chosen people. But during dinner, father was mostly silent and absent from our forced conversation, and we knew he was questioning God about our fate.

That night I slept on the couch in my parents' room. I heard my father sobbing as I never heard or imagined he could. Mama was comforting him quietly, but he kept asking, "What did I do, God? Why do I have to leave this place and go to the unknown? Did I kill or rob anybody? Did I cause suffering to any human being? Did I cheat or was dishonest with my customers or my workers? God, help my family, my children. They are so young and I wish them to get an education and live in peace!"

All these words resound in my mind; even after fifty years, they sound as if I am hearing them today.

It was dark in the room, but the moon lit us through the window and I could see the tears on father's sad, white face. He did not know I was awake. I was silent and stunned by this outpouring of pain and helpless prayer. I could not speak of this event, and this is the first time I have written about it. This was your great grandfather, Robert and Rachel, and you should know that he was a great human being. People who saw him in his last days told me that he fought for his survival and wanted to see his family -- my Mama and myself. He had already seen his son, Zoli, shot by an SS soldier in Auschwitz.

It was a long sleepless night, and my father and brother had to get up early to go to the synagogue. Zoli did not know anything of the night's sadness. He came to our room all dressed up to show us the new pair of shoes my father had made for him. He was always outgrowing his shoes.

I looked at my brother and realized how handsome he was. He was so thankful to my parents during these miserable days, months, and years.

We did not take all this for granted; we knew how much sacrifice and hard work was involved. But my parents did not expect gratitude, only some contentment.

The men left and my mother and I cleaned up the house, speaking very little to one another. Mama did not have to hide anything about Dad's outburst and questioning of God. She knew I had been awake and that there was nothing more to explain. We were anxious to hear the news from the synagogue, but we also hoped that during the holidays nothing would happen. The minutes slowed down, each one seemed to be an hour. I went outside several times but saw no one pass by. The village was silent.

Then I went into the garden and saw spring in full bloom. I smelled the scent of the buds of the lilacs, the cherry trees, and the apple trees, which were all in different shades of green. I loved this time of the year. Nowadays, I love autumn and its colors, but then I loved the spring. That spring was sad because I was saying good-bye all the time, and I was ready to cry every moment when I was alone. I felt like one who was old and had lost her childhood and beautiful teen years. I did not rebel. There was no one to turn against. My resignation, passivity, and sadness were inconsolable. But I could not bear it alone; when I was with family or friends I was somewhat secure, and we talked and fantasized about where and how we would continue our lives when the war ended.

When my father, brother, and Feri came home they told us that our deportation was imminent. The rabbi had been notified that in a very short time we should get ready. The authorities would give us at least three days before our departure. We did not know where we would be taken, what to prepare, how long our stay would be, or how long the trip would take, and our rabbi had no answers.

His grandchild, Manci, was my best friend and told me things that nobody knew. Some men had come to the rabbi's house and talked with him for a long time. When they left, her grandfather's face was as white as a tablecloth. He would have to go ahead of the group to prepare some kind of living quarters for us. We should be patient, the men told him: obey orders and accept everything without questioning. The secrecy was killing us, and we wondered how we could go on.

But the next Seder night had to be prepared. My father's mother was with us this night; she had spent the first night with Uncle Gyula, his five daughters, and his wife. Her black shawl covered her hair completely. Only her eyebrows could be seen above her beautiful eyes that looked somewhere else. I could not see what they focused on.

She sat down at the table, opened her Seder prayer book, and called on my father, "Yosi, begin," she said, "We have a lot to do tomorrow."

My father obeyed and began the Kiddush, but there was no pathos in his singing. It was as if God had distanced himself from the Jews of our day; he had only saved our ancestors.

The dinner was dull with very little conversation. My brother tried to crack a couple of jokes such as, "We won't have to worry about wandering in the desert because Transylvania is all mountains and rivers, and the spring weather makes it quite cool and just right for wandering."

No one could appreciate his humor. As the youngest member of the family, I stole the Afikoman and was waiting to be called on to bring it in from its hidden place. We drank the fourth cup of wine, and sang the story of the little goat that my Dad had bought with two pennies. We left the door open so that Elijah, the prophet could come in for his drink, and this second Seder night ended as joyless as it began. This was the last Pesach ever that our family would celebrate together.

The tension was tangible and our anxiety grew in the days that followed. We wished that something would happen, no matter what it was, just to end the torture of the cold and frightening present. We faced not only the omnipresent hostility of the Hungarian gendarmerie, but also the suspicions of the people of our small community. They seemed to be thinking now that perhaps the Jews were harmful to their society because the officials had gone so far as to isolate us, restrict our movement and communication with others, and to confiscate our goods. Maybe, they began to wonder, the Jews *should* be sent away. So when they finally heard we had been rounded up and they saw the trains in the station, they understood very well that they would soon have a village without Jews. A few of them were waiting to get hold of the goods the Jews left behind.

Our friends were hiding behind their curtains as they watched us. They watched old people, some of them unable to walk and traveling in peasant (third class) coaches sitting atop their small trunks; our middle-aged people walking fast between the coaches; our mothers holding babies in their arms, and fathers holding their older children by the hand. They watched our yellow-starred, branded people bowing their heads, ashamed of sins they had never committed and not knowing why this was happening to them.

Two days before, we had been notified that we should pack and be prepared to depart. We were told to bring food, but not perishables: flour, sugar, jars of fat, oil, marmalade, yeast, eggs, potatoes and a little smoked meat. No milk, cheese, or butter, because there was no refrigeration in those days and nowhere to store ice. We were also told to bring blankets, pillows, and enough light clothing for two or three weeks. It was the second of May, but the nights were still chilly and often rainy.

The Hungarians had told us we had two days, but they surprised us on May 3rd in the morning. Two cock-feathered gendarmes banged on our gate and marched into my parents' bedroom. Of course, we were not prepared, but they did not care.

The taller loud gendarme told us, "Get ready in half an hour, at which time we will take you out of your home and bring you to the train station."

They would not say where we would be taken afterwards. They said only that we would receive more instructions once we arrived at the station. They told us to leave all valuables behind and not to move or give away anything, or we would be severely punished. Leave the keys in the keyholes and extinguish the fire in the stove, they said.

They came back in twenty minutes with a crowd of Jews who were also waiting for us to join their ranks in front of our house. My father began asking questions. He wanted to know why his family had to leave our home that he had built, and for which he had worked arm in arm with his wife.

The official noticed that my mother wore her wedding band; he interrupted my father's question, took my mother's hand, and tried to pull off the ring.

Mama pulled her hand back and yelled, "Not this, officer! I've worn this ring for twenty-five years in a happy marriage and I will not give it to anyone!"

The man was furious, and cursed at my mother while continuing to pull at her hand. "I'll teach you a lesson, Jewish woman, which you will never forget! I'll take that ring -- you will not need it. You will not have a marriage, you will not have a home, and you will never return to this house. And don't bawl. Shut up!"

He pulled the ring, took it, and put it in his pocket in front of the five of us. Then he turned his shameless red face away, and marched towards the door. "Damn it," he said, "these Jews are still arguing."

"Follow me," he added, "and fast. The other Jews are impatient to get to the train station." There was no purpose in further discussion. They had the guns with the bayonets and we were their prisoners.

The distance to the station seemed to be many miles, but in reality it was only two or three. For us it seemed endless and timeless. From all the Jewish houses, two hundred families had joined us in this stop and go, sad, tragic, and hopeless march. I saw the puzzled faces of my friends and acquaintances -- all nodding as if to say, "So, we are all here." There was no difference between the rich or poor, healthy or sick, young or old, professionals or peasant workers. We were all there together.

The authorities evaluated our documents to determine our religion and it did not matter if there were intermarriages. The Jew was taken and the Christian remained. If the wife was Jewish, the children had to follow their mother, and there was no exception. If a man had been decorated for his heroism in the World War I, he was promised exemption for himself and his family if he agreed to convert to Christianity. This was a lie because in the final moments, these people were also deported.

Rachel and *Robert* -- this happened to your great-grandfather, Sigismund Knopfler, who was highly respected and had been honored with gold and silver military medals in the First World War. He was told that the Jewish laws would not affect him or his family, but it was a lie. His two sons, Leslie and Paul, were put into forced labor camps, while his third son was deported to Auschwitz, where all of them died. Papa Zsiga, Paul's father, and his mother, Mama Elizabeth, died in the gas chambers. His youngest brother, George, for whom your father is named, worked in a factory in Auschwitz. His campmate, Leslie Deutsch, told me about George's last days in the camp. Your dad's grandfather, Zsiga, died in Dachau.

Your father visited Dachau in 1974. Papa Paul talked to the dentist in whose arms his father had died. He told him that his father had whispered, "If my sons return from the Nazi camps tell them -- Leslie, Paul and George -- that they should go back to Judaism. We suffered enough for this religion; we may as well enjoy its values which have prevailed for five thousand years." He said he loved his sons and would pray for them. One day later he died of malnutrition.

When we arrived at the train station and saw the wagons, we rushed up its steps because we were exhausted from this terrible humiliating march and also because we wanted to escape the looks of our neighbors. Some smiled cruelly, enjoying this spectacle of a subjugated helpless flock of human beings. Very few showed sympathy, or even offered water to help us. But I was very thirsty, and asked one of our gendarmes to let me stop at a window for a glass of water. I told him I would not enter the house, but he still violently pushed me back into my lane with his rifle butt.

We climbed four or five steps into the wagons. We helped the old people first; then lifted their luggage after them. We carried heavy backpacks and wore three to four layers of clothing. There were just a few benches inside the wagons, and we teenagers sat on the floor or on our backpacks.

From that point on everything got worse and worse. The cock-feathered escorts yelled at us to settle down because we would be taking a long trip. They said we would arrive late in Somlyo-Csehi, our first destination. They said further instructions would come.

When we stopped at Sulelmed, the gendarmes ordered the men to step out and follow them. All the mothers and grandmothers began crying, "We don't want to stay without our men. We will go with them."

The gendarmes backed off; no one left the train, and we continued on our route. This was the first time I witnessed the effectiveness of our women's resistance. Perhaps the guards were afraid of too much noise and commotion, because in general, the Hungarian officials not only obeyed the Nazi orders, but they invented their own to contribute to our misery.

Late that night we arrived at our destination. Only a few petroleum lamps that were lit on tall posts revealed the chaos surrounding us. The place was a huge brick factory that was empty of bricks. The commander of this camp

CEHUL SILVANIEI — Vedere

was the infamous Jew-hater and sadist named Krasznai - - our former village mayor.

My house - showing the center of the village

Chapter Eight:
The Ghetto

The brick factory was our ghetto. Eight thousand people were living there like badly treated animals. My father told us that the term "ghetto" originated in Venice, Italy, where the first ghetto was built for Jews. In Venice it was an isolated part of the city where Jews lived in small houses and maintained small businesses under generally poor conditions. Merchants, teachers, and doctors lived there. A rabbi and a modest synagogue were the center of the community's spiritual life where they worshiped God and His laws -- the Torah.

Our ghetto was not even comparable to the original ghetto in Venice. Our ghetto was a place where people lived in subhuman conditions, and we were living this way in the Twentieth Century when a civilized lifestyle was improving hygiene and assuring better health for most Europeans. In our ghetto the orders were to destroy us, and we endured conditions not fit for human beings.

The bricks had been removed from the factory and so the ghetto administrators pushed in as many men, women, and children as they could. We were packed like sardines and only blankets were hung on concrete posts that separated entire families: each section was about ten feet wide and six feet long. A cracked flat roof about twenty or twenty-five feet high covered the factory. The bricks had not needed much protection from the rain.

One petroleum lamp provided light for three to four families. We also lit the candles that my mother had brought for Friday night candle-lighting, but we used them sparingly because we did not know how long we would be in this place. There was no bathroom, washroom, toilet or running water. To wash in the morning, we walked one kilometer to the Kraszna River where we collected water for cooking and carried it in two pails to balance our walking. Spilling even one drop would be a great loss. We stored the water in a barrel for the day. How many barrels would we need to quench the thirst of eight thousand people?

We were thirsty all the time; dehydrated from the heat and the salt we used to add flavor to our meager food. The administration provided soup at noon, but it was so bad that many families opted for one potato per person and some fat with which to prepare it. Mama boiled the soup in a dish we had brought from home. We had a frying pan and some matzo that we brought, just as our ancestors had when they fled from Egypt. Once a week a carriage with bread arrived from the nearby town of Somlyo, but we never knew the day or time of its arrival, so only the people who were present at the time of distribution got bread.

We tried to create some semblance of a civilized life in that miserable brick factory. We slept on quilts that we placed on the concrete floor, we put pillows under our heads and covered ourselves with blankets. For breakfast we had black coffee and, very rarely, some milk. The lack of toilets caused most of the problems. There were four latrines. The men dug trenches with benches above them. The guards examined our stools, looking for diamonds that we may have swallowed so that we would not have to turn them in to the officials. Every day the guards ordered the young men to dig and extend the trenches.

My boyfriend Ervin was ordered to dig, but he rebelled and confronted the gendarme, saying that he would not work to construct such a shameful and subhuman place. He said that he would build an enclosed toilet where we could have some privacy. The enraged gendarme ordered two men from the crowd and told them to tie Ervin to a high tree branch by his arms until he was no longer able to endure the pain, and fainted. The gendarme said that the rebel should then be cut loose from the tree to set an example for all: whoever would disobey his orders would get this punishment. He promised us there would also be other variations of torture for those who refused orders.

By sheer accident, one of the men called from the crowd to hang Ervin was my father. I saw the sweat beads on his forehead and the blood drain from his face. I had to watch Ervin faint and then be cut from the tree. I cried and suffered with him. I thought nothing worse could happen to us. We were hungry, thirsty, humiliated, and without hope that our conditions would improve.

My Uncle Mihaly was one of the desperate few who wanted to give up and end his life. Mihaly was my mother's brother and had married my father's youngest sister, Emma. They had two beautiful boys, Misu and Bandi. They were my favorite relatives and my sweetest cousins. Misu had been in fifth grade at my school when I was in tenth. We used to see one another in the schoolyard at lunch break. He had come to my school from his home in a small village and was living with strangers as a boarder. He was quite young to be living on his own and he needed me. I was proud of him and kept abreast of his accomplishments: he was at the head of his class. In March, after seven months at my school, he was sent home just as all the students attending Jewish schools had been. Bandi was only nine years old. Now, in the ghetto, his father seriously considered ending the agony of their lives and the possibilities of their frightening future.

Both my grandmothers and most of the family met in the barracks where my Uncle Mihaly lived. We gathered at sunset and the atmosphere in the barracks was morose. Of the children, only my brother and I attended this morbid meeting as the others were with friends in a nearby tent. My Aunt Emma was sobbing while my uncle explained why he wanted to die. There was no future for his sons; they were homeless and had no hope of work. His business had been taken away, his savings extorted, and he and our family had lost our freedom of speech. Armed men were dictating unjust rules and offering the Jews neither an explanation for what was happening nor any idea of what the future held for our families. And we Jews could not rebel.

All the secrecy and lying and his fear of the unknown had made him so hopeless and depressed that he urged the rest of us to follow his steps. I was so frightened by his determined face and by his words and gestures that I began to cry out loud, and all eyes fell upon me who had been unnoticed until this moment.

My father took my hand and led me out, calling to my brother to follow us. He talked to us softly and calmed us down, saying that nothing would happen; that we were together and we would stick it out. So we went to our place in the brick factory and waited impatiently for our parents. When they returned, they comforted us and said that everything had settled down, and that my uncle had been persuaded to wait with the rest of us for a better solution.

Unfortunately, the next day my father's brother came to our barracks to inform us of more trouble: something that had been rumored was now confirmed. Uncle Gyula worked in a tailoring section of the ghetto. Along with two or three other men, he repaired and pressed clothing for the German and Hungarian officials. Next to them was the room in which those who hid valuables were tortured. We were very curious about the "work" done in this building. Jews, some wealthy, some not, were invited to the room without knowing why. There they would be told that the officials knew that they had not turned over all their valuables to the banks, and that the officials knew that there were valuables hidden on their property and in their neighbors' homes. The Jews were told that this was their last chance to turn over everything they were hiding from the authorities. They were assured that after the war their belongings would be returned to them.

The officials threatened the Jews by saying that they had methods of eliciting the truth if they did not volunteer it, and they did not wait long to demonstrate these methods. Needles were jabbed under their fingernails and their lower backs were whipped with leather belts. First the men were tortured, then the women. The soldiers pressed the breasts of these women until they screamed and confessed, even if there was nothing to confess. The next day they were taken to their village to dig up the ground and uncover the valuables. If there were none, more beatings and punishment followed.

Uncle Gyula heard all this from the sewing room. He soon convinced my father to hand in one trunk of our goods, mostly linens -- my dowry. Both my cousin Ika and I would be of marrying age soon, and the hope was that after the war there would be something left to give us.

The trunk also held two gold bracelets which we hoped could be sold easily after the war so that we would have enough money for food.

Our parents remembered the poverty after World War I; my father's family in particular had suffered a great deal. There were eleven children and a sick father who eventually died. There was no breadwinner. My father's oldest sister, who had been a dressmaker, died of Spanish Fever right after the war, and my father had to give up his dream of becoming a singer and worked to support his family.

Despite these memories, Uncle Gyula did not hesitate to tell the ghetto leaders the location of his own and his brother's trunk. He feared the torture he heard through the walls both day and night. Later, my mother and I found out that my father refused to confess to the money he and my mother had saved for their children's education.

Late at night in the darkness, we sat on the concrete floor and discussed our present condition, as we seemed to have no future. We shared news of friends who had been beaten or had fainted and kept their secrets despite the torture. We spoke of those who had tried to escape, only to be recaptured. I knew two youngsters, Paul and Palma Weinberger, who managed to escape in the back of a truck that carried bricks from the brickyard. They are still alive today in Israel. I know of no one else who considered this. I would never have considered leaving my parents; it would have been a tragedy for me to leave without them. My father kept telling us that as long as we stayed together, we could find a way to overcome our difficulties; somehow the war would end and we would start a new life together.

Then we were flooded. Two days of rain paralyzed us and we could not even step out of the brickyard. The mud from the surrounding mountains and hills quickly moved into our habitat, because it had no walls. The water rushed in from every direction, so we stood in the rain and, for the first time in two and a half weeks, had a good shower. It was the end of May and it wasn't cold, so we tried to enjoy the moment and forget our worries about the future and the hardships of our present situation.

The guards circled us and whispered that soon we would be transported to another destination where we would no longer be parasites on the country -- parasites that produced nothing and merely ate and slept. We would be put to work on farms because the farmers were away fighting the war against the Russians. They said that Jews were slaves, and we would stay slaves as long as we lived. Get ready, they said, the official word will come soon.

We were undergoing terrible conditions and were also deeply afraid of the unknown. Our food supply was greatly diminished. We had almost emptied the bags of flour, sugar, dried beans, and jarred tomatoes that we had brought with us -- food my mother had prepared for the long winter months.

It was the third of May when we entered the ghetto, and most of our winter provisions had already been used. We had been expecting a fresh crop in June, of course, but we brought everything we had. During our last week we had run out of many things, so we traded with family and friends: jam for potatoes, onions for flour, etc. All we had left were onions, some matzo, cocoa powder, and chicken fat. It was a terrible combination of food, and it had to last at lease four days because, as we had been told, we would then be taking another trip.

One day we were told to pack a small bag, and to choose its contents carefully. Everything else was to be left neatly in the brick factory. The administration would collect everything and store it until we returned, they said. We left blankets, pillows, pots, pans, and clothing. The women were allowed to take two or three blouses, and the men could take work pants; everyone had to wear sturdy shoes that could hold up to heavy marching. We could also take non-perishable food and bottles of water. All day we sorted our remaining clothes, trying to decide what we needed most: soap, toothbrushes, and paste, towel, eyeglasses, three changes of underwear, and warm sweaters.

My brother brought the small pillow he liked to have whenever he was away from home. Zoli was a very private person -- neat, polite, and subtle. He had been deeply hurt in the ghetto on the third day we were there. He was standing in front of the brick factory while Mama was trying to light a fire under a brick to warm some water for tea. She saw a patrolman, but could not warn my brother of his approach. Without reason, the patrolman slapped my brother hard under his right eye, which was his blind eye, and it was tender and sensitive from the unsuccessful operations he had endured.

My mother told me that Zoli turned around, red with anger, ready to hit the patrolman back, but my mother grabbed his arm and stopped him. She feared retaliation. Zoli suffered great shame, and never forgave Mama for making him swallow the injustice of this brute. His life in the ghetto was made even more miserable by this experience, and he was bitter and hopeless throughout. I saw this same, hopeless expression when we were separated at Auschwitz, when he looked at me for the last time, without a smile.

I am not certain if it was May 27th or 28th when we were ordered out of the brick factory. We gladly obeyed because we hated this place. We did not know what was waiting for us, but we did not think it could be worse. We walked to the train station like a herd of animals, and were prodded to go faster. We went without speaking or complaining. Then we saw the cattle wagons. We thought it was incredible that these wagons were to be used to transport human beings. Before we were moved onto the train there was another search of our bags, pockets, underwear, panties, and bras, by women who volunteered for this important job. They did their work thoroughly and rudely, some of them penetrating our bodies to search for diamonds or money that might be hidden in cotton, in handkerchiefs, or in our panties. It was humiliating and painful.

After the war the ghetto chief, Dr. Molnar, was put on trial for the crimes he committed and ordered others to commit, he was accused of this searching procedure which resulted in suffering and infections both in the wagons, and for many of the following days in Auschwitz. I know of two girls who were menstruating at the time of the search, and the intrusion caused excessive bleeding. This was not the only accusation against Dr. Molnar as he was responsible for the terrible conditions in the ghetto. The lack of cleanliness and the impossibility of good hygiene risked the health of eight thousand people who were forced to live in the brick factory with open latrines and no decent washing facilities.

After we had been there for two weeks there was a rumor that Dr. Molnar and the chief justice of the region would visit the ghetto to check on the well being of the people there, so everybody created a petition listing the most important conditions necessary for us to exist in the brickyard. In the petition, Mrs. Gal, a very respectable widow who had been the wife of a physician, asked that milk be provided at least once a week for children less than four years of age. As two important authorities approached, she kneeled down and placed the petition in front of her where they could not avoid seeing it. They came to the spot where she was kneeling, saw the paper, kicked it, stepped on it, and passed by the crying Mrs. Gal. One named László Krasznai said, "These damned Jews try to live, eat, and feed their babies. They even think of petitions! We can never get rid of them!" He and Dr. Molnar were tried for their atrocities after the war. Krasznai was condemned to life imprisonment for his actions, and Dr. Molnar was sentenced to five years, and died in the fourth year of his sentence.

My mother and I have argued many times about the exact date of our leaving the ghetto. Mama said it was the first of June 1944, but I think it was at the end of May, the 29th, 30th, or 31st. We did not have a calendar and the guards confused us with the preparation for the train's arrival. They had told us that we would be given one week's notice, but they only announced our departure the day before it happened.

Secrecy was one of the weapons they used to prevent panic and rebellion. The guards did not tell us where we were going, when exactly we would leave, or how long the trip would last. If we asked any of these questions we were "lucky" if only a slap was the punishment. More often, we were punished much more severely. "Keep kneeling on those pebbles until the train comes!," was a more likely response. Sometimes we were told something along the lines of, "Pack your luggage with clothing enough for three days. You will sit a lot, stink, and suffer. Get used to it! Take with you enough food for three days, if you have any left. For three weeks you have stuffed yourselves; now you will be hungry! But that is all right. And you won't have enough water to quench your thirst."

The guards' words to us were always peppered with cursing and condemnation. "The Goddamned Jews want to know everything, even their futures," they laughed.

There was so much hatred and sarcasm in their constant yelling, that I begged those around me to stop asking questions. In this way we could pretend to ignore the importance of these matters. We could not trust any answers they gave us, anyway. Who knew where the truth lay in all their hateful rhetoric?

I began now to really worry about the silence of my boyfriend, Ervin. He did not care anymore, trusted no one, and suspected the worst. His face was lifeless, and his eyes stared hopelessly into the vague unknown. My father was the only one who tried to keep our spirits up. He kept telling us that for that time, at least, we were together as a family, surrounded by friends, and if we worked, they would surely feed us until the war ended. And he predicted that the war would soon be over, and whispered that he knew the Nazis would lose. I was so confused and so impatient with the situation in the ghetto, that I thought nothing else they could do to us could be worse.

My uncle's (Mihaly) wedding

My cousins, Misu and Bandi

Chapter Nine: Auschwitz

On the morning of our departure, it was unusually stuffy in the ghetto. After many rainy days of mud sliding down from the hills around us, it began to dry out and vapors were created which, like light smoke, rose into the brick factory. We lined up starting in front of the building, but the endless line of people snaked alongside and then around to the back. We carried our backpacks which held food for three days (onions, canned foods, tomato juice, and some bread) and their heavy weight pulled down our shoulders. We also wore a lot of clothing in layers so that we would be able to change when we got to wherever it was that we were headed.

One of the guards remarked that despite our meager food supply in the ghetto, about which we were always complaining, we were fat. But of course each of us was wearing two pairs of panties, two slips, a dress, a blouse, and a coat or jacket. We were unable to take along more than one pair of shoes or boots on our feet. Some old ladies took their fur coats and carried them with the lining on the outside, hoping that the guards would not notice. If they did, they pulled the coats off the old women and left them without any coat at all. Fur was expensive and the guards took the coats and put them on a pile, promising that the owners would get her coats back when they returned from their "work."

We all wondered where our "work" would take place. Besides the backpacks, we each carried a small piece of luggage, the size of a briefcase, with our name on it. Inside was a small blanket (to make us feel as though we had a bed), some toiletries such as soap, and a toothbrush (toothpaste was forbidden because they thought we might hide diamonds in it), a small towel or cotton napkin, eyeglasses, some sanitary napkins, and a few aspirins.

Everybody was checked thoroughly. All women, adolescent girls, and little girls were taken into a tent one by one. Then a female volunteer (often a nurse) searched every part of our bodies with her fingers. They used magnets if they felt anything suspicious. If a girl refused to be searched, the nurses called in a male guard to assert his authority; this humiliated and devastated us.

We were abused, ridiculed, and hurt by these brutes. I often wondered how they were trained for this job. I could not believe that what I witnessed was spontaneous brutality. The government was careful to use men from other regions so that they would be hostile toward us and there would be no neighborly rapport or friendliness. When I was searched I was very embarrassed, so I tried to cover myself with my hands here and there. The woman laughed at me and then made fun of my red angry face. She said I had a pretty figure and should be showing it to men. I asked her to let me dress, as others were surely waiting outside the tent. While I was quickly pulling my shirt on, a guard came in and, to humiliate me, lifted my shirt with a leer on his face. I asked him if this was included in the orders regarding the search or if he was just taking the liberty of making his own rules for Jews. He said he did not need special rules; he was entitled to satisfy his desires with the Jewesses if he wished. He said that he was a young man full of sexual desire but would not degrade himself and make love to a Jewess.

That was the end of our conversation, and he lowered the hand that lifted my shirt. I turned around and ran out of the tent feeling disgusted; tears were forming in my eyes --tears that only my mother saw. My mother entered the tent right after me and was seen only by the woman. She searched my mother under her bra and between her legs. I found this out only after the war. That time, my mother wanted to spare me her embarrassments and hurt, so that what they did to her would not hurt me too.

This thorough search went on for hours until every person returned to the brick walls and lined up for roll call. Around three o'clock we were pushed along to the wagons that had been waiting for us all morning a half a mile away. We had seen the train tracks when we carried water from the well.

The trains we had seen were cattle wagons, so we had no idea that they were meant to transport us to the unknown. Seventy people were piled into each wagon with two windows secured with iron bars. The windows were so high up that only horses could have reached them for air. There was not enough room for so many people to sit down at once, unless the surrounding people were standing. Sleep was impossible. In one corner was a big pot, like a garbage can, where we were supposed to relieve ourselves. Four or five women or men, depending on who was using the makeshift toilet, formed a human wall to provide some privacy. I could not urinate for days; I was ashamed that Ervin would see me.

The Hungarian gendarmes locked the doors from outside after they piled the old and sick together into the wagon with the young and the babies. We heard the heavy iron bars clicking, and then the huge lock closing.

It was getting dark when we pulled out of the station. How many wagons were there? How many people were left in the ghetto? We did not know. I looked around for my family, and saw that they were almost all there. The only ones missing were the family of Uncle Mihaly, my mother's brother, who had wanted to kill himself his family when we were in the ghetto. They lived in a different section of the brick factory and must have been in another wagon. I never saw them again.

My father's mother suffered terribly in our wagon. She had difficulty breathing and the heat of seventy bodies, the smell, and the hunger, tortured her during the entire three-day trip to Poland. We only realized the next morning that we were leaving Hungary.

Our train suddenly stopped and gendarmes entered again to search for any hidden gold that we might have kept in spite of all the searches and the constant warnings. The gendarmes wondered why we would not want to give the Germans what belonged to them. They said it was in our interest to give everything -- money and valuables -- to them, because we would get it back when we returned. They were ordinary thieves in uniform.

We did not have anything valuable with us, so they left frustrated and yelling. Some people outside the train attempted to bring us some food and water, but the angry guards would not allow it. They emptied the toilet barrels, but would not let us descend from the train. Finally, they locked the wagon.

Night came and we could hear the cries of children for food and water and the old people praying to God. To make room for the old and sick to sit, my father stood most of the time. I saw his profile in the moonlight and he was not optimistic anymore. He only spoke when I struggled to get close to him. He was near the window and he lifted me up to breathe some fresh air. He smiled and tried to comfort me with a hug. "Soon it will be over," he said. I did not know how soon it would really be.

During the three day journey, he ate only onion and some bread. Better food, such as tomato paste and marmalade, he left for the children. His beard had grown, and I saw gray that I had not seen before, mixed in with his black hair. I felt sorry for him and my heart went out to him. I remembered the night in our house when I had to sleep in the same room with my parents and overheard their quiet voices when my father had sobbed. Ervin's family was in the same wagon with us. His grandmother had fainted in a corner far from us, but we only heard and saw the commotion around her. Ervin was sitting near me at the time and could not get through the overcrowded wagon fast enough. I do not know if she died then, because, besides my mother and myself, not another of the seventy occupants of that wagon returned to relate her fate.

I met Ervin's sister, Blimu, in Stuthof at the end of August in 1944 and she told me that some prisoners wearing striped uniforms took her Grandmother from the wagon on a kind of stretcher and she hoped they took her to a hospital because she was very ill. Who knows what happened to Blimu after we were separated? We never heard from her again.

With the monotonous noise of the train in the background, Ervin was comforting me by saying that I was strong and basically optimistic, so I could fight for my life. He wasn't confident, however, that he had the strength he would need. Because of his political activity he had secret information and knew what we could expect.

He said that if he thought he would be around to prove it to me he would make a bet that the Russians would occupy Romania in August of 1944, or he would eat a big soda bottle. This is how sure he was. Of course, we know from history that he was right about this. His prediction was amazingly accurate.

As he spoke I could not see his eyes or smile, but I could tell how serious he was. We both became quiet and sad. The train pulled on and never whistled so as not to draw attention to its curious appearance and its people in cattle wagons. Only the hungry childrens' voices interrupted the quiet. I recognized little Gabriel Borgida's voice crying, "Give me some bacon and bread, Mama, you promised food."

Ervin and I were sitting very close to each other holding hands, hugging, and kissing as if we never wanted to separate. During the last couple of hours I felt that this should never end; we belonged to each other soul and body. It was the kind of love, desire and attraction that only comes with the passion we felt.

My brother interrupted my thoughts. He did not know what was going on. He asked what I was thinking about, and when I told him, he bit his tongue, pinched my arm, and said I was thinking only of my feelings and was using the few remaining minutes and seconds to enjoy my life and had forgotten him. He continued to curse and yelled his rage against the world. I had never seen him like that before, and unfortunately this picture has stayed with me all these years because I never saw him after that night, not even in Auschwitz.

When the train stopped, a guard opened our wagon and I saw the local men at the station. I asked the guard, "Wie heisst diese Stadt?" (What is the name of this town?)

His replied, "Auschwitz. You'll never forget it."

Men and women were separated. The men had to leave first. My father took my brother Zoltán by the arm, and Zoltán never looked back at us. He just walked like a somnambulant. Then my father looked back at us, waved lightly, and smiled as if to say, "See you later." I could not see his warm eyes because it was dark and we were already being pushed to step out of the train. This is my last picture of my father. I cherish it and keep it vividly in my memory. This unique human being was good, honest, and loving.

After the men were all off the train we again heard shouting, "Los, austräten, schneller." (Get a move on, get out, faster, and leave your luggage on the platform.)

This time they did not say that we would be getting anything back. Some men who looked like worn out prisoners whispered words in Yiddish, "Be quiet and look well, head up, healthy posture, don't cry." Although it was dark on the platform, I could see their ashen faces in the light of a high lamppost nearby.

Everything was chaotic. There was shouting, crying, and confusion that could not be handled. Guards with dogs surrounded us, and I had to empty my bladder right there near the wagon. I could not hold it any longer. The prisoners took the barrel of excrement from our wagon and passed near me so nobody noticed. A disgusting smell came from the barrel.

The inhumanity of this still stirs in me hatred against the Nazis. I felt so humiliated, but I did not have time to feel sorry for myself. Quickly, one shock after the other took my full attention.

The wagon was emptied of the remaining women who looked like ghosts, pale and sickly. Most of the young people jumped from the wagon without realizing that it was very high and had no steps, and many were bruised or hurt. Their knees landed on pebbles and they tried to clean their clothes and legs of the dirt.

The prisoners kept telling us in Yiddish to stand up and follow the line, that there was to be a selection. We were so numbed by the events, we followed without asking anything. Then a strong SS man, armed and holding a stick in his hand like a great orchestra conductor came towards us. He pointed the women right or left without saying much. To his right he directed the old women, younger women holding children in their arms, and those holding children by the hand. Sometimes he pulled a child from a woman and pushed it into the arms of an older woman. At the time, none of us knew his reason for making the selection. We just speculated that the young women would work while the older women would watch the children.

Then, it was our turn to be selected. Mama and I were pushed by this powerful, smiling, and cursing giant into a line of adults who were all over fifteen years old and appeared strong enough to work in slave labor camps.

Josef Mengele (we found out later) was the man who selected us. He had good eyes even in that dim light. He did not waste a second to argue or to explain why my mother was pushed to his left while all the other women on our wagon were directed to his right. We did not know that this little motion to the left meant life and a chance to survive.

Mama did not understand why she was the only woman among the young people and wanted to go the other side on her own; she said "look Blimu's mother is there on the other side and Hedi's mother." She thought they had made a mistake. My friend and I pulled on her, grabbed her arm, and forced her to stay with us. If this is a mistake, we thought, then let it be, because at least we will have one mother with us. She was forty-six years old, but she looked thirty-five and was very pretty, tall, strong, and vigorous. With all the clothing layers she wore, she looked heavier, yet walked easily in her ankle-high boots. (We had been told in the ghetto to wear our sturdiest shoes for our future work, but unfortunately, my mother's shoes did not last until the end. When the Red Army liberated us, a Russian soldier saw her run-down wooden shoes. He gave her soccer shoes that he picked up somewhere, but she had swollen legs all during our trip home from East Prussia.)

A different group of guards came and took charge of those of who had been sent to our group. They counted us and led us in lines of five in the opposite direction from the others. While passing by large iron fences, the guards warned us never to touch the metal because high voltage electricity ran through them and would kill us.

We asked what was happening to the men and to the others who were being taken in the other direction, and they answered calmly, "You will see them tomorrow and be able to talk to them through the fence." We believed them and were looking forward to the morning.

We saw a huge gate with an inscription we could not read that night, "Arbeit macht frei" (work makes one free), that inspired us for the few minutes until we realized how ridiculous this slogan was.

We passed by huge barracks and smelled smoke, and then we saw a big chimney from which the smoke rose, blackening the sky. My mother said that it must be a crematorium where they burned dead people. She assumed that there were no cemeteries and that if anyone died in this place they were cremated. The whole place was dark and frightening.

It was probably around midnight but we could not be sure because none of us had had a watch for a long time. Here and there we saw some ghost-like figures coming out of barracks, running barefooted to some less visible point near the barracks, squatting close to the soil, and then quickly running back, hopefully having avoided being seen by the guards. I knew right away that they must have the same problem I did. We did not have toilets, and it was terrible.

I squeezed my mother's arm to make sure that she was with me. After twenty minutes of marching on the stony road, we saw a somewhat different barracks with a light at its entrance where three or four SS men stood smoking, chit-chatting and laughing. They did not even look at us or seem to notice the newcomers.

We were directed to enter this building one by one in a long line. My mother did not let go of my hand. It was hard to enter through the door like that, but we did it. A long hallway was emptied for us and we were ordered to undress completely, and to proceed to the next room holding only our shoes in our hands.

Five women worked feverishly shaving the women's hair. They did this non-stop in twelve-hour shifts. They had their hair and wore striped uniforms. My turn came very quickly. My fine, dark, warm-brown wavy hair reached my shoulders. I was ordered to sit by a woman who pointed her finger to the first chair. Without looking at me, she took her instrument that still had the last woman's hair in it, and began to shave mine. Tears streaked my cheeks as she sang and mercilessly continued nonchalantly shaving, circling the crown of my head. In those five minutes I felt violated and stripped of my femininity forever.

I asked with a trembling voice, "Why do you sing while you do this brutal work on me?"

She was furious at me, slapped me, grabbed my shoulder and said, "You snotty bitch, what do you lose"?

Your hair? My parents were killed in front of me in Warsaw three years ago. I lost everybody, family and friends. I worked in a ghetto and in three camps until I got this job. This is the only way I can keep my sanity. I was a singer. I love to sing!" And she finished by shaving my pubic hair. Then she was ready for the next woman, but looked at me and said quietly, "Try to get out of Auschwitz anywhere you can go!"

I ran to my mother who still had her hair. She looked around and asked my friends, "Where is my child? Where is Klara?"

I was standing right next to her, but she did not recognize me, so naked and shaven was I!

Now it was her turn to go and she kept repeating, "What did they do to my beautiful child?" (Later on we found out how much better it was to be bald because it prevented lice from infesting our hair for a couple of months.)

While we were standing on line waiting to be shaven, three high-ranking SS men were walking up and down looking at us and cracking remarks about our naked bodies. They looked at me, too, and said I was too young.

The girl next to me was three years older than I, tall and very shapely. One of the SS men said she would be good for the front line in the Ukraine. I had no idea what he meant, but the two other men were definitely against what the other had said and remarked, "Sie wird schnell tot sein" (she will die soon), and they walked away from us.

Later, we saw three girls from our group marching in front of the SS men. They were stronger, heavier, and unshaven. Now we knew that their task would be to service the soldiers at the front before they were killed, too. In the concentration camps Nazi guards were severely punished if they had sex with a Jewish woman, but on the front lines unfortunate Jewish women were used to satisfy the sexual urges of the soldiers, some of whom had been at war for years.

By that time, we were numb, speechless, and emotionally drained. But then we were directed to soak our shoes in a trough on the side of the room before going to a shower room that had disinfectant water.

My boyfriend Ervin's picture was hidden in my shoes, and this fact woke me from my numbness. I put only my left shoe in the trench to soak, and in this way I managed to save his picture for a long time. We were ordered to leave our shoes and to put them on after the shower.

About five women went under the shower together. We were given no soap or towels. In three to four minutes we were disinfected. It was a cleansing we needed after nearly four days sweating sickly perspiration in the heat.

We dried while we searched for our shoes in the crowded entrance hall. Some people had two different shoes; some had two left shoes or two right ones. Mama and I found our shoes easily because they were so different from the others. They had been beautifully handmade by my father and Feri -- the only employee of my father to stay with us until the end. He was Jewish. Even in the ghetto he lived in our cubicle like a family member. He had not been able to return to his parents in Alba-Iulia, Romania, because the borders had been closed in 1940.

Our first night in Auschwitz remains the worst time of my life. By midnight we were two hundred women, naked and shaved everywhere, being checked for hidden valuables. Still wet from the shower, we were led to a huge room full of clothing. Dripping all over, we were finally given some dresses, but nothing else. I was given a long gray dress that later was useful because I could rip from its length to put something on my shaved head, or whenever I could, cut a piece to use as a pad while I was still menstruating for the next three or four months. I grabbed a pair of panties from a hidden pile. My mother was given a beige, double-breasted coat-dress with no belt. I grabbed a black cotton slip for her that she also used as underpants. She was upset that she could not have a bra: she weighed one hundred and eighty pounds and wore a size 40D-cup bra, and now she would be very uncomfortable when walking.

I put on my shoes and felt Ervin's picture in it. It gave me such comfort. Although it was slightly wet, for a long time I could still see his face. Often, SS women tried many times to take away my shoes for their quality but they could not wear them. They all had much larger feet, so I had those shoes till the end of the war.

Finally we got dressed, and Mama and I looked at each other. The first look was a shock-followed by a smile. We both remembered a crazy old lady in our village who we now resembled. This old lady lived near the synagogue in a little one room apartment and lived totally in the past. She was not violent, but quite neurotic. She dressed very oddly: she had hats like Marie Antoinette, very long colorful skirts and sandals in winter and summer, and she sang the same old songs day and night. Everybody laughed with her when she told stories of her childhood and her life as a courtesan (she had never been a prostitute), when she said she had as many lovers as the freckles on her face.

We started to sing what the "pretty woman" -- as we called her -- used to sing, and it was tragic-comic. We looked around and saw the others looking just as ridiculous as we did. I hoped my father would not see me the next day, because he would be devastated seeing us like this, but we couldn't think about this too much.

I told Mama that I would get revenge for all of this after the war. I'd tell everybody how they pushed us as if we were animals. I would eat so I could exist, and I would fight for our lives in spite of this torture. She seemed to hear me, but only later showed me that she would try to help me in this fight.

The next order came fast. We were told to stand in lines of five, which was the standard way of marching to work, standing on roll call, waiting in the morning for food, or waiting for the various selections. I thought we would never again be able to walk alone without four others. Mama and I were always with three sisters, the Blau girls: Irene, Lucu, and Hedi.

Hedi was my friend and classmate. Later she died in Riga, the capital of Latvia, in the concentration camp known as Kaiserwald. We thought it was scarlet fever that killed her. She had been in the sick room (there was no hospital) with other girls who first only had lice but while there, had picked up other contagious diseases, like scarlet fever. They were all taken out one morning and we last saw them in the back of the truck driving them away. Blonde Hedi – now with her shaved head -- was very pale in her dirty black dress, and she was waving to us saying she would be back tomorrow. But the truck came back with only the dresses of the girls who had disappeared.

What had happened? How could they have allowed this to happen? Where were they now? We didn't know. The two sisters were inconsolable. Lucu and Irene went into a deep depression; they were sick almost all the rest of the time in the camps. We were always afraid that Lucu would be taken with the sick people like her sister, so Irene fed her, covered her when she was in trouble, and worked for the two of them, and that is how they survived.

This first night in Auschwitz, however, our column was ordered to march in the darkness of the night like ghosts wandering on the shards of an unlit place, and we were followed by a one-armed guard. He made demands such as "Schnell!" (Fast) and "Maul halten!" (Shut up), and we stumbled here and there on the hard pebbles that cut our feet if we were barefooted.

By this time, we were dead tired as it must have been 2 a.m. or later. Many terrible things had been happening to us in the last couple of hours!

We passed a huge barracks that looked just like the other one which we had passed, which had closed doors. Then we got to one that had an open door through which only two to three women could enter at a time. We could not see or hear anything; when our turn came, we entered and were stunned. In the semidarkness, we saw hundreds of bodies lying close to each other on the floor – speechless and half asleep -- staring at us newcomers.

We were ordered to occupy the empty parts of the floor where we were to sleep until morning, when they would yell, "Austr@ten!" (Get out!) for roll call. We filled in every little space until no one could move. Our group consisted of at least six hundred newcomers. But we had no sooner lain down than we felt thirsty and many of us went to the toilets. The Kapo, the woman who pressed us into this large place, yelled, "Just get up! Sneak out of the barracks! If you can't hold it, it doesn't matter. You'll see outside where to go -- four or five at a time."

Mama and I walked out, trying not to step on anybody's head as we moved to the exit. Outside in the pitch dark we looked for latrines, but there were none. When we couldn't hold it any longer we found some grassy spots where we crouched and emptied our bladders. We used some long leaves for toilet paper, and it was horrible. We ran back to the barracks but couldn't find our place, so we settled silently where we found a spot on the floor near another group. Mama prayed and I fell asleep, pushing myself very close to her.

We were awakened by a loud voice. It was our Kapo yelling and cursing, "Get up, you lazy trash, get in lines of five."

This was the 5 a.m. roll call. There was no washroom and no water and therefore, no need for toothbrushes, toothpaste, soap, or towels. So we went outside, following the other women who had lived in the barracks. There we found our Hungarian group and ran to them because we felt more secure among them. Nobody had slept well and we all complained of the hard floor and how impossible it was to turn over with so many bodies pushing for a little more room to extend their tired arms and legs.

We were warned to be quiet, stand still, and wait for the roll calls, so we could not argue too much. SS women moved in front of our lines counting by fives and forming us into groups of hundreds. It took long hours to organize this flock of miserable women. If we got tired of standing, the Kapos reminded us with long sticks to straighten up. That really hurt.

Somebody came with a bucket, paint, and a brush, and put numbers on our backs. I had 51455. (Our group escaped the tattoo; that was used only for those who stayed longer than a week in Auschwitz.) The paint had to dry, so we had to stand there longer, and a rumor spread that we would be given breakfast at around eight or nine o'clock.

I suppose it was around that time that we were told to go one by one back to the barracks and take our ration of bread, one plastic dish for coffee or bran soup, and a wooden spoon. Then the Kapo there filled our dish with coffee that was artificially sweetened and pushed us inside where we could sit down and eat our breakfast. The other inmates warned us not to eat all our bread because that one thick slice (one inch) was our allotment for the whole day. We did not believe it and we were very hungry, so we ate the whole thing at once. If we had saved our food, we would have risked having it stolen from us anyway. Today I know we should not have judged those people who stole food. Hunger can overrule one's honesty, ethics, or self-discipline.

For half an hour everybody was quiet and wondering what would happen next. We asked the girls who had come there before us. They were Polish Jews whose ordeal had begun four years before. We met very few of them and they hated those of us who had just come and were complaining, so they mostly ignored us and answered our questions reluctantly.

They urged us to accept any work that was given to us, just to get out of Auschwitz. They warned that this was both an extermination and a concentration camp. Of course we did not understand fully what this meant, and we were so preoccupied with the present misery, filth, heat, thirst, hunger, and diarrhea that we could not think of anything else.

The Kapos called us again, and this time we stood in front of the barracks and the SS men and women randomly pulled out big strong girls from our rows, and sent them to work. In the evening they came back exhausted from doing road construction. The rest of the group did nothing, and just stood for hours. By 1 o'clock or so the sun was so hot above our shaved heads that some of us collapsed from dehydration, most suffered from hunger, and a diabetic girl went into a coma.

Then we heard there would be some food. A big container (like a garbage can) containing pink-colored food was placed in the middle of our group of one hundred, and the Kapos tried to ladle this thick soup into our dishes. We were so afraid that there would not be enough when our turn came, that everybody pushed ahead and each of us took a little bit of soup with our own wooden spoon. The Kapo beat us up with her ladle.

When we tasted the soup, it was so horrible that only a couple of us could eat it. It was supposed to be beet soup with some kind of starch, corn starch or some chemical powder that tasted like uncooked flour and was very salty. Beets only colored this food -- there were no beets visible. Then came the thirst, but there was no water to quench it.

We did not go back to the barracks until the dark evening. SS men came and counted us. Again, one by one, we extended our dishes to be given our food. Some liquid - not soup - with parsley in it, was our meal that night. We did not need water to wash our dishes, because we licked them to get the last remaining drop.

God was good to us that night: A heavy rain came and the roof of our barracks was leaky all over. We drank the rain water that poured through the smoky, dirty roof.

We only cared that it was wet. I will never forget this long day and the other five that followed with little variation: beatings at the food lines, diarrhea that sent us running to newly discovered latrines, and a strong determination to get out of there.

That very day we heard more and more rumors that we did not believe about gas chambers, a crematorium, torture, and other SS cruelties. We were very restless already and eager to have some work that might bring a change in this horrible situation.

Based on our experiences since we were taken from our homes, both the fear of the unknown and that it could be worse with each passing hour constantly frightened us.

Auschwitz

Auschwitz - Birkenau

Chapter Ten:
The Road to Riga
(Kaiserwald)

By what was probably the seventh day (I do not know for sure because the nights blended with the days and sometimes the sun was covered with clouds), we were selected along with a group of about one hundred fifty other Hungarian women. Except for my Mama we were aged from sixteen to twenty-five. After our legs, hands, and feet were examined thoroughly, we were told to step aside and wait. We were told that we would get some work, that we had been of no use for a week, and had just eaten and taken up space in the barracks. We were each given three rations of bread, a half pound of knockwurst, and a quarter-pound box of solid marmalade. They told us that this food was to last a minimum of three days and nights and "nicht fressen" (we should not eat it all right away). We were to die of hunger, but we must work until then.

After waiting for two to three hours we were taken on foot to the train station about five miles away. There we were herded into cattle wagons, each of which held about seventy people, just like those that brought us to Auschwitz. The only difference was that we had water in these wagons, and once a day the train stopped in the middle of nowhere so we could empty our bowels and bladders. Unfortunately, we could not limit our body functions to just that one stop. Poor Lucu, who had had diarrhea since the ghetto, lay in her excrement for three days and could not control her body.

We all suffered from the heat, filth and unforeseen misery. Mama prayed and would swallow only the bread we had been given. The girls and I tried to talk about our lives before: boyfriends, parties, books, and poetry, but after each sentence somebody's stomach would hurt, and others thought that we were ridiculous to even hope to have that life again because they thought we would surely die soon and that the whole world had forgotten us. Even God, we thought, had closed His eyes on our suffering.

As the train continued to roll on the tracks, the monotonous noise seemed to be rhythmically repeating my thoughts, which were always: let us live, let us live, let us live. Where we were going and how we would stay alive, I did not know. There seemed to be no answer or solution. There was only sweating, suffering, and napping.

The rhythm went on and on. If the train stopped, we ran to the door, the locks opened, and armed SS men watched us jump off the train and run to find small bushes behind which we could hide our embarrassment at our undeniable animal urge to let go. Of course, we had no toilet paper, and could only wipe our bodies with leaves or grass. And there was no possibility of finding a way out. All we could do was try to cope with all the hunger and dirt, and wait because we were in a tunnel, and there was no light at the end for us.

Mama prayed silently. I saw her lips moving, but I could not tell if she was speaking Hebrew, Yiddish, or Hungarian. I interrupted her, and she told me that she was speaking all three in her prayers for us and for our family. I heard her mumble my brother's name and ask God to give him patience because she worried about his impulsiveness. And she prayed that my father would have work that would allow him to rest his legs, because she knew that, with his vascular problems, he would not be able to stand for hours. She also worried about her mother, and wondered if, at the age of seventy, she had any chance of surviving. And her younger brother, Mihaj, had a short temper and would not tolerate any abuse from human beings.

I listened as my mother talked to God, begging, crying, and asking Him to help us as He had always helped before. She asked Him to work miracles and reminded Him of Exodus. She sat motionless; only her eyes and lips expressed feelings. Then she looked at me and thanked God because at least we were together.

Babuci and her mother were also in our wagon. We were the only lucky ones as even in our misery, we appreciated having our mothers who, however, had not known each other. Babuci and I had been friends since we began attending the Jewish school in 1940.

Sitting on the floor of this disgusting wagon and thinking of our problems then and our situation now, I wished I had only those complaints again, instead of this bitter life. If we had known that the Allies had landed in Europe and the Russians had encircled Hitler's occupied territories, we would have had some hope and inspiration to go on and stick it out. But we were kept in the dark, as good news for the Jewish people was well hidden.

We had not seen a newspaper since May 3rd, before we were taken to the ghetto. There, some people had hidden books, parts of books, poetry, and loose sheets torn from books, and they had brought them to the brick factory. Some afternoons we got together in one of the corners and tried to do math with the leadership of the older students, or we recited poetry, but in Auschwitz we were living under such subhuman conditions that we could not even think of what was going on in the world. It was like a silence before the storm -- guessing without optimism.

Now we sat on the train. Mama put her hands on my head to see if I had a fever. She worried because my eyes were too shiny; yet, she knew that all that was happening to us was enough to make anyone sick.

She listened intently as some outside noise disrupted the silence. The train slowed and then it stopped. We heard a voice on a loudspeaker say that we were soon arriving at our destination and should prepare to step down from the train, get in lines of five, and listen to orders.

The train was rolling still when the wagon doors opened on an astonishing view: gray sky, gray yards, dark gray barracks and not a soul in sight all the way to the gray horizon. A siren sounded and SS men in green uniforms stepped out from the barracks. They walked to our train to meet the new supply of two-legged animals who would produce the necessary goods for Hitler to win the war.

They yelled and pushed us into rows of five and directed us to the barracks of this place. It was around five in the afternoon we thought, because we smelled dinner being prepared. It was, as we discovered later, the smell of potato peel soup, to which our stomachs would rebel because for three days, we had had no warm food or anything that could satisfy our hunger.

When we entered the fifth barracks we were surprised by its cleanliness and by the wooden two-story bunks with some blankets on them. The SS woman, Caroline, woke us up from our naive hopes, however. In her harsh, manly voice, she said, "Don't touch anything until you are told. This is not a shit-house like a Jewish home. Here we have German neatness and discipline."

Caroline was a political prisoner and her punishment was to be with Jews. She was miserable and because of this she was very cruel with us constantly yelling and beating us like we were dirt.

The first night she hit my mother because she had started to unfold a blanket. In the beginning we were to sleep two to a twin size wooden bed. It happened that Babuci and her mother were on the lower level, so we could whisper to each other and share our misery. Later, when more transports arrived, they placed one more person in the twin size beds, but somehow we managed to stay just the two of us. That night, like all the others, we were exhausted and hungry. If we could, we would had gone to bed right away and slept forever, but instead we were ordered to go outside and wait for dinner. After an hour, some girls collapsed from fatigue.

The blows of the SS womens' clubs awakened them. "The first five come in and be prepared with the bowls you brought with you from Auschwitz. When you get your portion, go to your bed and eat it. Don't eat the whole piece of bread. Leave half for your breakfast or you will starve till noon."

We approached the huge can where Caroline ladled out a thick potato soup made mainly with peels, some carrots, and some starch that Mama could not identify. The soup was hot and salty and the piece of bread was one inch thick and hardly enough for one meal, yet Mama forced me to save a piece for morning.

When everybody finished, Caroline said there was some left over for the youngest. I did not hear her say this, but Mama did, and she rushed to get me more food. Caroline laughed at her and yelled sarcastically, "You are the youngest?"

She hit Mama hard with the ladle so that her dress was full of stains. Mama did not cry, but her face was red, and I began to cry because she had been hurt because of me. This was our first day in Kaiserwald (the Kaiser's Forest) in the outskirts of the town of Riga.

We fell asleep in spite of this incident; we were so exhausted. At five o'clock in the morning, a siren woke us. It was dark outside, but there was a lot to do. We rose quickly and rushed to the cold shower room where we washed without soap or towels; then we put on our clothing to dry. Luckily, it was June and warm outside.

We stood in lines of five to be counted over and over by different SS men and women. They told how to stand and how to work (although we did not yet know what we would be working on), and they kept telling us and emphasizing the importance of our work for the Third Reich.

Breakfast finally came, but all we could see was the long line for coffee, one piece of bread (for the day), and some bran cereal that was thin and tasteless, although sweetened with saccharin. This was the breakfast served in all the concentration camps, and, as one could expect, it left us hungry for the rest of the day -- unsatisfied, irritated, and hopeless.

We were given ten minutes to eat and drink our coffee and get back to our place in line for "Austräten," the march to our workplace. Fifty yards from the barracks was the road we were to travel for three months: it consisted of broken-up Jewish gravestones. We had to step on letters or very short words that we could decipher if they had dots on them. Babuci and I had had four years of Hebrew in our Jewish school, and we had a good base of Bible knowledge and Jewish history. Walking on these stones was like stepping on our grandparents, our families, our fellow human beings. We felt as though we were desecrating the Ten Commandments and we thought of the instruction to respect our elders so that we might live a long life.

At that time, however, we did not want to live a long life. We were preoccupied with our constant hunger and only hoped to eat a whole meal once more, to sleep on a normal bed, to clean our teeth with a toothbrush, and to shower with soap and a towel. As we walked to the place where we would work, we were so humiliated and crushed that we could hardly function. The road was about two miles long and we were not allowed to speak, to share our thoughts or feelings.

On the first day we were not told the purpose of our work. From six o'clock at night until six in the morning we dismantled huge batteries and placed the components into four piles: aluminum, wires, copper, and the residue of the batteries. The precious material was sticky, dark, and rubbery and had to be scraped from the walls of the blackened aluminum. We were to scrape every bit out so the Nazis could use it for gunpowder. We were later told that ammunition was the most important and most necessary product for winning the War.

In the morning, another group came at six and left at six in the evening. At night we saw them leaving looking exhausted, pale, and filthy. We tried to ask some questions, but they could hardly speak: although they were Hungarian Jews, they were frightened to talk to us. They managed to advise us to follow orders and work if we wanted to live. They were apathetic and hopeless. It was June 1944 and they had only been in the Nazi camps for one month. In Auschwitz we had some hopes of getting out. Now, being in Riga, our perspective on life was grim.

Still, Mama said, "God will help," so we held hands and our hope was revived.

Our Scharführer (leader) was an older man who did not wear a Nazi uniform and looked kindly. He was not frightening and did not carry a gun or a rubber stick. He did not yell, but was firm in his orders. His assistant was a German Jewish woman, Ellen, who was strict but willing to explain our complicated work. After all, recycling was very important in the poor German economy of 1944.

Ellen wore a thick pair of glasses and her face showed the suffering but also the pride she felt in not giving up. We learned later that she had lost her three children when she was taken to Kaiserwald; she did not know where they were, but she was determined to find them again. For that purpose she was willing to endure everything to survive.

She was patient with us and urged us to produce or we would be doomed. She said that we were lucky to have this old man as a supervisor and said he was "not that bad." The problem was the night work.

We worked without any break until ten or eleven at night when it was still light in Riga, almost like daylight, but when the darkness came, we were ready to fall asleep. By midnight we were so sleepy we could not hold our heads up. Ellen walked to each group and warned us that we should not sleep. She poked her fingers into our backs, pushed us with her elbows and touched our fingers, telling us that she would be punished if she could not make us produce.

The Scharführer saw her desperate attempts, looked at me, and called me to his desk. I was frozen with fear. What had I done wrong? I had only slept a minute, I thought, and no one had seen me. I stood in front of him, trembling. The old man looked at me with understanding eyes. "You little girl," he said in German, "you must sing in German."

I murmured "Jawohl." (Yes.) I was searching my memory for two or three German songs which my father had taught me. He believed in singing a song in the language in which a composition was written. I remembered a Mozart song, a Schubert song, and Lehar's love song, "Dein ist mein gantzes Herz," (My whole heart is yours) but I was not sure if I knew the lines correctly. He looked down at me, smiling at my surprise. Then he looked up again and said, "When dark sets in outside and you feel that your regular sleeping time has come, start singing. Even if the people around you do not know the words, they will hum the melody with you and this will encourage them to sing along. They will join you and they will not fall asleep. They will work. Otherwise, I will have to beat them every night to keep them awake and force them to produce."

His good intention to avoid using physical punishment was the first spark of humanity I had seen. Maybe not all Germans considered us animals and slaves, I thought, so I immediately responded to him saying, "Danke, ich werde sicher singen." (Thanks, I will surely sing).

You remember, Rachel, when we sang a lot to your brother, Robert, when he was a baby. He was not a good sleeper and I took him in my arms when he cried. I sang two lullabies, Mozart and Brahms. You stood next to me and sang along. My singing voice was nice; I inherited it from my dear father, who was a great singer. Those were the songs that saved sixty women from being beaten during our night shift in Kaiserwald.

God bless my father's memory. He was such a wise man.

At the end of the night, the old man secretly gave me a few slices of bread that I took to my group of six and shared with them. It was more valuable to us then than a million dollars, and I was very proud of it.

But there was another event that affected my mother's and my fate even more. One night the main machine that recycled the aluminum broke down. The old man called in a mechanic, Henek, to fix it. Henek was also the old man's chauffeur when he needed transportation between the factories in the concentration camps, as well as his handyman, and he knew a lot of what was going on in the camp. Henek listened intelligently and rarely asked questions so as not to invite refusals.

He came to us that night and quickly fixed the machine. I watched him speak respectfully to the old man. Then he looked at us and stopped at our table. He saw that we were bald newcomers from Auschwitz. He said something to the old man and approached me while I was working. I felt miserable and ashamed of my baldness when this handsome young man in his early twenties stopped in front of me and greeted me quietly like a gentleman.

He said that on Sunday he would try to meet me in our barracks because Caroline, the Kapo, was an acquaintance of his from Germany. Even though she was bad with us, she was friendly to him when she needed him to do some work in the barracks. He was one of few men who could enter the women's camps on Sunday, when we did not work until 6 p. m.

On Sundays we were supposed to clean ourselves and our places, wash the huge dormitory and have one hour of rest behind the wire-fenced barracks in the sunshine, if there was sunshine. This is the place to which he would come if my mother would give me permission. I could cry now about how impressed I was with the civilized, warm, polite words this young man spoke to me.

It happened on a Thursday and the anticipation for Sunday was so exciting that even today as I write, I can feel how a human encounter revived me. I prepared questions to ask. I wondered if I could tell him about the last time I had seen my father and brother, about how cruel the SS had been to us, and about how hungry I was all the time. I wondered what it would be like if I cried in his presence. Would he think I was a baby, or would he comfort me somehow?

To improve my appearance I ripped a five-inch strip of material from my long gray dress which I used as a turban to cover my head to try to hide my shaved hair. My dress was so long and loose that I was able to take another inch for a belt so I could show off my waistline. By that time I had lost five or six pounds and was really thin. I had no mirror, but in this barracks we had some tall windows, and I could see my silhouette.

On Sunday we came back early from work, about five o'clock in the morning, and I went to bed right after my shower so I could sleep a few hours before Henek came at noon, but I was not really able to sleep well because I was so excited. I kept talking to my boyfriend Ervin in my dreams. I was telling him that Henek is an older guy and that no one could take his place in my heart.

Maybe Henek could do something for my own and Babuci's mother who were always praying, although God seemed to be hiding from them. They would not eat the bran cereal given to us in the morning because they felt it was food for pigs and not cereal for human beings to eat.

They suffered silently and refused to eat any of the extra bread we tried to give them; they said that we two girls must have everything to eat that we could get.

In my dream Ervin understood and he told me that he knew I loved him, and he wished me luck surviving this ordeal. He reiterated what he had told me when we were in the wagon to Auschwitz: I was strong and hopeful then, unlike he, who had already given up in the ghetto.

I finally fell asleep but woke up when Caroline yelled, "Los. Los. Kaffe holen (quick, get the coffee)." To wash again in the daytime was forbidden, because those who worked the day shift needed the water, so we put on our shoes, pulled on our dresses, grabbed our bread ration with some sticky lard smeared on it, and our sweetened coffee that looked like dirty dishwashing water. This was our Sunday meal.

While we stood on line for this breakfast, Henek arrived, walked in between the lines of prisoners and watched Caroline while distributing the food and yelling at us. I heard him asking Caroline if he could have some of the leftovers because his rations were so very small. She understood the joke and even smiled at him; it was a smile that looked odd in her wild, angry looking face.

Henek watched us with our wooden dishes and spoons. We had no need for knives or forks and we drank water from the single outside faucet used by thousands of prisoners. We never had coffee and soup at the same time, so one dish was more than enough. We rinsed it in the washroom with cold water and did not think of infections or bacteria. Instead, we thought only of when we would have our next meal. The hunger numbed every nerve of our brains; our thinking was focused only on getting food, feeling cold or hot, seeing light or dark.

It was a nice day outside the barracks. We were separated from the other barracks by a wired electric fence. There was no communication allowed beyond this fence. We were told that there were some male prisoners working in the administration: doctors, dentists, shoemakers, and barbers. They worked for the SS guards some days of the week.

In July I had a terrible toothache, and, thanks to Henek I could go to a dentist -- a Jewish man from Riga, a prisoner himself who treated me without pulling out my tooth. He was alone because he had lost all of his family. He gave me a book of Shakespeare plays in German in the Gothic letters. I knew how to read them, but it was hard to understand. I was very proud of this book. For a long time it was the only source of intellectual stimulation I had. Just the fact that I, Klari Deutsch, was the only one who had such a treasure, and that I could, in whatever spare moments I had, see the written words of a masterpiece, made me happy. One day Caroline saw me reading it, even though I kept it hidden under the blanket, and she tore it from my hands so I never saw it again. That was in late August when the Russian army was coming.

My dear grandchildren, you must pardon my wandering mind. There are so many things that I want to tell you and I am constantly sidetracked while I am writing the details.

For me, all of these were so important in the daily misery of
my life that I appreciated any little bit of luck that helped
me to go on to survive.

When we had our food in hand, some of us used to
go outside and sit on the ground with our backs against
the wall of the barracks, but that day Mama and I saved
a place between us for Henek, who followed us instantly.
He was the only man among hundreds of women and
girls who sat leaning on the walls. I felt like a girl again:
I was getting attention from another human being -- a
boy, or rather, a man.

Henek smiled, took my hand in his and talked to
my mother. He told her that he was happy to know us
and offered whatever help he could. He was so amazed
to see a mother and a daughter together. His own parents
and a sister had been killed in front of him in Hamburg
in 1940, and he had been expelled from his house and
taken to work. He was twenty years old at the time, in his
second year of studying engineering at a university, and
looked as if he might be useful to the SS soldiers.

Since that time he had been in many concentration
camps, working as a mechanic and chauffeur, driving all
kinds of vehicles: trucks, jeeps, and luxury cars. He had
learned how to exist in his many different circumstances
despite the obstacles. He wanted to live, not only as
revenge, but also to try to help the Jewish people survive
Hitler's aim of destroying them.

In this first conversation he told my mother that he
liked me very much and that after the war he would like

to spend a lot of time with me and perhaps ask me to marry him. This was so remote to me that I did not tell him anything about Ervin. I only told him later when I saw how earnestly he meant this. He became very sad, but understood that Ervin was my priority. He wore thick glasses, and his big brown eyes were full of tears. He pulled a red scarf with handwork on it out of his pocket. It was triangular in shape and he put it on my head and looked at me with admiration, saying that this would cover my head until my hair grew back. He gave me a toothbrush (not new, but clean) and a big piece of bread with margarine on it. Our friendship grew each time he came. I would see him in our workplace when we had a problem with the machine. Everybody knew by then that I had a boyfriend who cared and helped us as much as he could. I liked him and respected him. He taught me how to cope with difficulties.

One day, two hundred new girls arrived in our barracks to be placed in our bunks as the third person in each bed. My dear cousin Ika was among them. We jumped from our beds and took her to our bunk. We gave her a slice of bread, and then questioned her about the family.

She was my Uncle Gyula's oldest daughter. There were five girls in their family, and she was one year younger than I, so we were friends also. Ika and her family had been in a different wagon coming to Auschwitz, so I did not even see them at the selection upon our arrival. Ika told us that our Grandmother Luisa, her mother, and her three younger sisters were pushed to the left, and she did not know what it meant. Her sister, Touyou, who was forteen years old, was with her in Auschwitz for three weeks. But then Ika was taken to East Prussia to work in a factory, and she was separated from Touyou in spite of their trying to stay together. All of us were happy that at least we had Ika with us but Ika was crying and laughing in sorrow and happiness. We had much to talk about. It seemed incredible that we had undergone so many experiences just since June.

We arranged somehow that Ika would come to our factory and work the night shift with us, but when we stood for roll call, she was pulled out from the line and ordered to go with her group. So we saw each other the next day in the morning when we returned from work.

At noon, all of Ika's group were put into three trucks and driven out of our camp. We thought they were being taken to work in fields outside the camp, and we expected to find them back in the barracks the next day. But at six o'clock in the afternoon we saw one truck come back with the clothing of two hundred girls. What had happened to them?

Henek told us the next Sunday that they were annihilated because one of them had scarlet fever. We did not know how they were killed, and we would not even guess. Henek would not say more. It was unthinkable that we had lost Ika. Later we learned that they most likely had been gassed in trucks and taken to a crematorium or buried in a mass grave.

Losing Ika saddened us terribly. What else could we expect? Every day, every hour, brought another tragedy.

I mentioned earlier that three girls, the Blau girls (only one, Lucu, is living today), had completed our five-person line ever since Auschwitz. We were friends until the very end in the concentration camp in Riga. Lucu and her sister, Irene, babied Hedi. They washed her dress and Irene gave Hedi her own ration of bread whenever she could, but Lucu had been constantly sick since Auschwitz and could barely take care of herself.

Hedi was the tallest and prettiest: blond, and full of zest and hope. She and I were talking while marching to our work one evening, joking quietly and dreaming. We were outlining what we would like to eat now and what we would eat tomorrow, if we could. We counted our imaginary money and argued about what kind of ice cream we would buy -- chocolate ice cream was always more expensive than vanilla -- but her parents spent more for food than mine, so she could have whatever she wanted. (My father used to spend our money on musical notes and books, so I had to buy vanilla ice cream instead, because it was cheaper.) Then we laughed out loud at our incredible conversation.

Hedi had been spoiled as the youngest member of her family and she enjoyed it without guilt. Her smile was omnipresent, and showed her beautiful teeth in an expression of full contentment. Of course, she looked so different to me now, with her long blond hair shaven and the bones of her skull protruding. Hedi kept touching the bones of her head and laughing at them (of course, we could not see ourselves).

Hedi hated the cold water and tried to avoid the shower after long sleepless nights. We always yelled at her, and her sisters pushed her to undress and shower, but she laughed and escaped many times. Her pale face was always marked by the dirt of the batteries, and, whenever she washed it, she looked dirtier than before! Whenever we found some recycled paper towels to dry ourselves, she hated that, too. She used her dress to dry herself.

Two weeks before we left Kaiserwald, Hedi got sick. She had a fever and her whole body was shaking. Irene had to tell Caroline, our Kapo, that her sister Hedi, #55514, needed a doctor. Hedi was taken to a so-called hospital three blocks away from our barracks, so we were able to see her from a distance of fifty yards beyond the wire fence when we went to work. Hedi told us that she had to be kept separate from the other patients because she had scarlet fever. Her rashes made her whole body look like a map, and she could not stand to look at herself. She said she never liked geography anyway and we all laughed, but we were devastated. We could do nothing and we knew what had happened to Ika.

Sure enough, on Sunday a covered truck came and took ten girls from the hospital. Hedi was standing in the back of it in her black dress, more blond than ever, waving to us and saying she would be back after four weeks; they had told her it would take that long for her to be cured. The arc of the cover of the truck curved around her head like an aura, and framed her figure like a beautiful painting in a museum. I will never forget the sight. These memories still haunt me so vividly that I shiver.

We followed the truck until it disappeared, and then went to our work crying silently. Lucu and Irene were sobbing and were unable to work. We covered for them by working harder and the forewoman turned her head; she knew the cause of our suffering. The old man, the SS, ignored the scene for a while, but then he ordered us to get back to work. He said it would help if we worked.

"Who is next?" we wondered. "What is next?" These were our constant questions.

The filth, the malnutrition, and the emotional distress slowly demoralized everybody, even those who tried to live. Henek came that evening and read the tragedy on our grief-stricken faces. He knew how I felt when I had lost Ika, and that now I had lost Hedi, too. He came to my table and embraced me, disregarding the presence of others. He wanted to comfort me.

At midnight, the Russian bombers came. They started early, and many more circled around our camp and, of course, Riga. They brightened the whole sky with "Stalin candles," settling, it seemed, on the top of our barracks and telling us, "We are coming! Soon you will be liberated from the darkness and misery, though you cannot escape now."

Nazi airplanes chased "the candles" away. The Nazis wanted to destroy the Russian planes in their last efforts to win the war. No bomb ever fell on our camp. The

Russians must have known that this was a prison camp holding Jews and non-Jews, so they did not aim at us. Some of us prayed that they *would* bomb us and finish our hopeless situation. They showed up almost every other night, but the more they came, the crueler the Nazi guards became. The Nazis took all their frustrations over losing the war out on us as if we were to blame -- pushing us harder and cutting our bread rations daily.

One morning in the middle of August, as we were going to the shower room, we were stopped suddenly and ordered to listen to an SS woman while a prisoner distributed soap. "You dirty Jews don't know how to wash. You spread all kinds of disease among you. Soon you'll kill us all!" she yelled.

We were so frightened that we could not wait to get under the shower and we scrubbed hard until she yelled again, "Don't use the entire soap in one day! Are you all crazy?"

The guards chased us out of the shower. When we examined the soap in our hands, someone noticed the letters "RJF" on it, and the rumor started that these German initials stood for "Rein jüdisches Fett" "Pure Jewish Fat." This was an unbelievable, terrible shock. Most of us did not believe the rumor, but Mama and I never washed with that soap again, so we began collecting the sand from under the train tracks and scrubbing with that. It scratched us, but it cleaned us.

When we got back home in 1945, we again heard the rumor about the soap. Some Jews brought home the soap and buried it in coffins because they considered it the bodies of human beings which deserved a ritual burial.

The atrocities we knew about -- gassing us, using our hair for mattresses, extracting our gold teeth and sending the gold to Germany, using our bones for the preparation of glue and combs, using our skin to make lamp shades -- caused us to believe that the Nazis would use our fat to make soap.

Henek was our only contact with the outside world. He knew things; he even got a chance to read newspapers when he went to Riga with the SS people. One day, he came to our factory before our dismissal at five in the morning. He was very excited and could hardly control his face enough to conceal the secret he held. He sat on the edge of our workbench and handed me a red paper. Intrigued, I looked at him. He told me that as soon as we washed there would be a huge roll call; there would be no breakfast and no sleeping because there would be a selection. He said I should use the red paper for my mother's cheeks so she would not look pale or sick or old. The Nazis were emptying Kaiserwald because the Russians were approaching. The young and healthy would be selected and transported by ship somewhere to work but he did not know where. The most important thing was to look healthy and act young.

We did not believe him. We thought he was trying to comfort us. A ship for Jewish prisoners? It was unheard of! He told us that he had seen forklifts with loaves of bread, and boxes of lard and marmalade. Surely the Nazis would not sink such a ship filled with food! But they would kill us if they did not need our work. Little by little he convinced us to get ready for a very serious selection which would mean life or death. He had no idea what would happen to those who stayed behind in Kaiserwald. He had to say good-bye then, but promised that after the selection he would come to our barracks to see us before we left on the ship. His whole story was so incredible and unexpected that we were really puzzled and frightened about our future. Henek said that he would like to try to join us on the ship, but this was beyond his power. He got up and hurried away with tears in his eyes.

At 5:30 a.m. we cleaned up the place, and packed our one dish and wooden spoon. Then we stretched a minute to prepare for the next shift. It was the hardest time for us because our night shift would have to sit for twelve hours on one wooden bench. Lately, we had been lucky, because our work was often interrupted by the bombing of Russian attacks by Stalin's Candles. We would stand up, go to the door, and watch them falling from the sky. It was spectacular.

We stretched waiting for the order to step into the washrooms. We thought about the place where we had worked every night for the past two and a half months, and thought it was not so bad compared to the unknown that awaited us. At least the old SS guy did not beat us, and if we produced the amount he required, he left us alone. We were sixty hungry girls -- his slaves. Yet he appreciated our work and did not torture us.

There were other groups -- at least fifteen others like us -- and they complained all the time. When we all returned to our barracks in the morning they would report that they were tortured if they did not work fast enough. They would be forced to kneel for two minutes on sharp, broken aluminum, or made to stand on one foot for minutes on end. We had been luckier than the others. It was only required that I sing to keep my group awake. I looked back to the old guy, bowed to him gratefully, and he smiled. A human smile from an SS man! Incredible! Afterwards, he shouted "Austräten!" meaning dismissed and turned away. Perhaps he felt sorry for us.

Walking back on the broken tombstones to our shower room was a reminder of how mortal we all were, and how our dignity had been destroyed. There was some commotion in the showers as everybody talked about the selection. We feared any change now because we expected the future to always be worse that what we already had experienced. We washed nervously and rubbed ourselves with sand to clean our skin carefully and give our cheeks some color. I colored my Mama's face with the red paper that Henek brought me -- she looked so pretty, but she had lost so much weight that I was worried about her and I could not bear the thought of losing her. I decided that if they tried to separate her from me, I would try to go with her. Somehow, I would outsmart the SS.

We were still wet from the shower when we dressed. It was warm outside, so we dried as we stood at roll call. At 6 a.m. sharp we were standing in rows; about four rows of five women stood ahead of me so no one knew that I was the daughter of the oldest prisoner at the front line. We were all hungry for breakfast, which we would only get after the roll calls and the selection. Our faces were burning from a sleepless night and the excitement of the unknown.

Then I heard yelling. The SS men and Carole were ordering the prisoners to straighten their rows, and be disciplined while waiting. They reached Mama's row. She was visibly older than the other four girls, and one SS man looked at her and demanded, "Wie alt bist du?" (How old are you?) My mother said she was thirty-nine, though in actuality she had turned forty-six in June.

The SS man got angry and said, "You are not even thirty-one, but you want to die so you won't have to work for us to win the war. You don't believe in our victory!"

Holding a stick in his right hand, he lifted my mother's dress and pointed to her thighs, saying to the other SS, "This woman who is so full of energy chooses death; she lies that she is old." He pushed her onward and said, "You won't die yet; you will work for us until you're dead."

When I heard this, I almost cried from happiness. "Thank you dear Henek. We were prepared for this and so we live for who knows how long."

One hour later our group was through with the selection. Only a couple of women who were sick were selected to "go to the hospital." The rest of us stood in line for breakfast. We ran to get coffee, and I grabbed Mama's hand so hard that I almost broke it. I did not want to kiss or hug her because I worried that the SS was watching us and would change their minds if they saw our happiness. Yes, we knew this from experience. The SS was so brainwashed that they forgot that even they were human beings.

We went to sleep at 8 a.m. and were so close in our bunk that I heard my mother's breathing and quiet crying. We did not dare speak. Babuci, who now slept in the lower bunk, did not speak either. She was happy that her mother, who was younger than mine, had also passed the selection. I could hear them praying and expressing their gratitude to God.

After a couple of hours of sleep we were ordered to get up and get our things together in bundles. We collected our dish, our wooden spoon, and nothing else. We were to leave the bed prepared for new arrivals, get out of the barracks, and stand outside for a final count.

There were a few among us who already knew that we would be taken to Riga's harbor to embark on a merchant ship. And there was Henek, with his eyes red from not sleeping at all the previous night. He looked around carefully and came as close as possible to say good-bye to us. He reiterated his belief that we would not be dropped in the sea because he had found out that the ship for our transportation had been loaded with bread, cans of lard, and some marmalade to keep us alive for the work that awaited us. He did not know where we were going, but he assured me that after the war he would come to Hungary, that we would survive, and that he would marry me if I chose him and not Ervin. It sounds so naive, romantic, and incredible now, but those words were so real to me that they gave me strength and support to continue to fight for life in an unknown future. We looked at each other, cried, and waved for the last time. I never saw him again. He saved Mama's life and mine too.

We were ordered to step out and march. We saw for the last time the road covered with the fragmented Jewish tombstones, and the dark barracks where we had spent three months in slave labor living like poorly treated animals. I tried to think of the only humane German -- our foreman -- so I could hope that there would be someone else to help us to live a little longer. Of course, we were not allowed to share our thoughts, so we only looked at each other and marched according to rigid orders.

After about four miles, we saw in the distance the outskirts of the shipyard which looked like little dots on a cloudy sky.

In Riga it is always gray, even in summer, but we felt the heat of late August, and the strain of the fast marching in our weakened legs. We stopped suddenly and were able to get some water from a fountain near the road. We were only allowed one dish of water for each row of five people, and we had to share equally, taking only one or two gulps each.

Those in our row of five were very considerate, but we heard a lot of arguments and yelling: "Margaret, you only think of yourself! Stop drinking!" said Susie, as she violently pulled the dish from Margaret's hands, nearly spilling all the water. (Such an accident would have been a tragedy because the SS would not allow another dish to be brought.)

We were soon ordered to finish up and continue to the ship. We were excited upon hearing this because none of us had ever been on a ship. My mother was curious too, and wondered if our voyage would be like those she had read about in the stories she loved so much -- those she would tell us about in such vivid detail, that we felt as if we were right there.

Mama's cheeks were flushed and she kept saying, "I wish your father and Zoltán could be here. They loved the sea. Your father was on a ship in World War I."

She was rudely interrupted by an SS who yelled, "Was quatsched ihr?" ("What are you barking about?") To them the Hungarian language was "barking". We froze with fear. We could see tall buildings and thought we would be there soon. The sun was stronger than before, and we could feel the heat increase by the minute.

"Only God can help us," Mama said, and I looked at her in disbelief. I had stopped loving God when we were separated from my father. This is no time to philosophize, I thought, the goal is simply to carry out the orders.

The shipyard looked like a big city to me; there were huge warehouses, small houses, and many military tents. Many ships and smaller boats covered the sea, and I did not understand how they could all sail so near to each other. Our marching line slowed down and turned towards the biggest ship, which was about two hundred yards from the shore and the ramp. Forklifts were moving up and down, carrying merchandise to the ship's upper deck. We could not believe that this ship could transport people. All we saw were hundreds of huge boxes and garbage cans and a couple of SS men in various uniforms.

When I looked around I realized how big a crowd we were – eight hundred people, at least. Where would we be put? How long would we suffer on that ship if they did manage to pack us in like sardines? The answer was, "Wait till you get there," and we had to wait a long time. When some of us began collapsing, the others quickly picked them up so the SS would not notice; we knew the SS would not want sick slaves on their ship.

After an hour or more, the SS directed us to a steep ramp and we were told to walk up one by one and follow directions when we reached the top. Like sheep heading for the slaughterhouse, not knowing anything, we did not rebel or scream. There was nothing and no one who could possibly help us.

We did not stay on the top deck, but were led down until we were three or four levels under the sea. In each area, there were three tiers of fifty to sixty beds and each of those was to hold three women. I think of it now and wonder how we managed to breathe there.

There was one opening in our wing that led to the top and everyone wanted to climb up to get fresh air and look for toilets. That was a necessity, even if we were animals. Mama and I wanted to climb together holding hands, but we were pushed around and kicked from all sides until we had to let go of each other and separate. We did not find each other again until we went to bed. We did not find toilets either, so we went to the edge of the ship and used the sea.

By the time we got back our group was given some bread and lard and one slice of marmalade, as Henek had told us. Luckily, Elise, the third person in our compartment, a young girl from the neighboring village Hadad, saw our dish and asked for a portion too. She was honest and sweet and gave us all that she got from the SS women distributing the food, truly a heroic act by a hungry young woman.

We were on the ship for about three days, but I am not exactly sure. We were in the bottom deck of the boat and it was dark all the time, and there was one light bulb on the top of the three tiers of sleeping compartments and steps where we would go around, looking for a toilet or some place to empty our bladders. It was also a chance to breathe some fresh air, which we badly needed.

More and more coughing was heard in the sleeping area; we were suffocating. Elise coughed all the time. When I pulled and forced her to the top of the ship, she was so pale that it was scary. I saw other of us slaves dropping to the floor and lying there, barely breathing. I stayed with Elise until the SS ordered us to go back. "Don't die here," they yelled at us. "We have enough problems here with you parasites who eat but don't work."

We went back and found Mama sleeping comfortably alone in the compartment, stretched out and snoring.

Elise was so weak that she had to sit in the corner. And I remained until Mama turned in her sleep, her hand searching for me in the bed. I placed my hand in hers and she stayed asleep.

We ate in our compartments, too. We washed our hands with the coffee or water we had carried from upstairs in our dishes. Of course, we could not shower or brush our teeth. (I was the only one I knew of who actually had a toothbrush – the one Henek had given me). Most of the girls tore small pieces of fabric from their dresses, placed them on their fingers and rubbed their teeth with it when they had water.

The small piece of fabric was torn from a longer ribbon of material that was used as a belt on the uniforms we wore, which had a number on the sleeve or back. I needed a wider piece of fabric because I was one of the very few girls who menstruated for four or five months in the camps. I tore it into four or five pads and washed them while we were in Kaiserwald. Later it became even more difficult because we only had a pond in which to wash our clothing. It was more than a nuisance.

Rachel, I write this to you because I know how clean you are and it will be incredible to you to learn what the Nazis did to us, to me, your grandmother.

I had to take care when I sat to be sure that the blood would not show on my dress. Mama and most of the girls had stopped menstruating at Auschwitz. We thought the SS put something in our food to avoid this biological obstacle, but I guess it was not that because, I ate the same food as everyone else; it was likely the malnutrition the girls suffered, the weight loss, and the lack of vitamins that caused our menstrual cycles to stop.

Mama never had a period again after the war and, after six months of not having it, I wondered if I would ever have a child. These were serious worries for a seventeen-year old girl. As I said, it was a blessing not to have a period in the camp. The same was true of having our hair shaven. We could not have taken care of either in the camps. Yet, I did menstruate on the boat from Riga to Danzig. And at the end of August 1944, we debarked.

Those who survived the trip landed in Danzig (Gdansk) and we couldn't believe how beautiful it looked. I have never seen such beautiful flowers and plants anywhere else in the world. There were flowers with huge petals in every hue, some growing on low bushes and some on high trees; the leaves were like small green umbrellas protecting the buds from too much sun or insects. They were growing all along the river that flowed into the sea where our boat was.

We admired the view until the first and second groups of sixty were pushed into the bottom of a small boat. From there we could see only the tops of the trees, the blue sky, and the warm sun. It was a beautiful morning that stimulated new hope for our lives. We smiled and recited poems praising nature written by Hungarian and French poets. Even our hunger was put aside as we fed our senses with the beauty all around us. Hope was returning, and we thought maybe this place would be better. "Dum spiro spero." (One never loses hope completely as long as one breathes.)

There were no benches in the smaller boat, and all sixty of us sat on the bottom. The sides were four or five feet high, so we could feel the river water if the SS let us stand. The trip from the harbor to Stutthof lasted about half an hour. Judging from the position and heat of the sun and the feeling of emptiness in our stomachs, we decided it was about noon when we climbed out of the boat.

We looked back at the riverbank and that sight is still with me. No camera can capture the depth and colors of that view. After this, the days that followed were so disappointing. The events overrode the short time we had been in the boat when we had felt like human beings again.

We set off and marched slowly in lines of five, as we had been ordered. The two sisters, Lucu and Iren, hardly moved: their heads hung in sadness. They never had got over the loss of their sister, Hedi. Our fifth in line was now Leon; she had a great sense of humor even in the worst times. She was older than we were, and the only girl of five children. She wanted to survive and see them all again, so she did everything in her power to maintain her spirit and courage.

Leon had been a clandestine communist before the war, and had thought that Marx's ideology of equality would prevail and would solve the Jewish problem. She had belonged to the same communist youth organization as Ervin, but I only learned about this from Leon and another girl who worked with us. They felt superior because they had found faith in the communist ideology, in a secret that we did not know about, and they believed in it more than in God's help.

So Leon quietly sang the communist hymn, "International." "Arise ye workers from your slumbers; Arise ye prisoners of want." [Arise ye prisoners of starvation, arise ye wretched of the earth!] We related to the song because it was for the poor against the rich, but it also called for revolution, and as slaves, we could not rebel, so we told Leon to shut up unless she wanted to endanger our lives.

She smiled and looked down, mumbling, "Cowards, that's what you are."

Mama said, "Leon, we are slaves. They have the weapons. I want to see my son. You want to see your family. We must stick it out by bending for a while. Maybe there will be a time when we can rebel and you will be our leader!"

That did it. In that situation Leon respected only Mama. Deep inside she was a sensitive, caring, and warm person. Leon and two of her brothers survived. She married late, had one daughter who lives in Australia, but eventually was divorced. Leon was devastated, became sick and depressed, and died heartbroken.

There are so many little episodes that I want to interject. There are so many great human beings who cannot speak up and be witnesses for the millions of people whose stories were silenced by death. Each of these victims had a personality worth presenting because of what it can teach humanity. Each had values and shortcomings that we may not be aware of. What should we keep and what should we discard as we try to bring inner fulfillment to our lives and to future generations?

As my mother said in an interview with German television, "We survived to prove to Hitler that we are here forever. Jews did not die in vain. They have left traces in history, medicine, science, music, art, as in all aspects of human life."

Concentration Camps and Killing Centers

East-Prussia(Dorbeck, then Guttau)

Chapter Eleven:
Saying Goodbye

I stopped writing after the "Road to Riga" chapter because my mother became seriously ill. It did not happen suddenly, but it almost ended her life. For the first time it hit me that I could lose her. I know, Rachel and Robert, that you must be saying "But Grandma, don't you know that our great-grandmother is one hundred and one years old?" You are right. Yet, for me, if she goes, a whole world collapses. This is how I felt when she became sick and even after four weeks I chase away the thought that her leaving me is getting closer and closer.

Mama has had bladder cancer for about five years. Once, in 1994, her urologist, Dr. Siegler, found two small polyps and removed them without anesthesia. He said that one was malignant but that could happen at her age, and it was nothing to worry about.

Two years later I was in Budapest and Cluj at my Jewish school reunion when George called me and said that Imre, our friend, had taken Mama to the hospital. She had some bleeding and they operated on her successfully. George said that she would be home in two days, and that I should not worry or come home early; she would be fine.

So I talked to Imre who assured me that all was well, and sure enough, three days later I found her comfortably at home in Louisa's care. She was climbing the thirteen steps to her room, which is filled with pictures of you both, her beloved great-grandchildren. Your pictures are directly above the candle-holder where she prays every night, and the presents you have given her over the last eight years.

I was very grateful to Imre for acting so quickly in spite of the opposition of my closest friends, Carol, Nuna, and Miriam, who all wanted to wait for the surgical intervention until after I returned. Mama had five small polyps and one was malignant. The cancer has spread but the doctor comforted me by saying that Mama was still well and strong, and might have many years ahead in which to enjoy her very old age.

Mama was not as grateful to Imre as I had been. She did not want to have an operation. She was ninety-six years old at the time and doing light cooking, taking care of her needs, and reminding me of my responsibilities in the house and at school: of my appointments with doctors, of letters that had to be written, and birthday cards I had to send to family and friends. Her mind was alert and incredibly acute. There was no one who visited our home who left without admiring this old pretty woman who was always gracious and smiling. She was always up-to-date with what was going on in the world and would ask everybody questions until her inquisitive nature was satisfied.

To live with my Mama for nearly my whole life, except during high school and my first year of college, has always been a challenge and still is. The security that only a mother can give, even throughout my forty years of married life, has never lessened. Her keen criticism is blunt but constructive. She says that dealing with my shortcomings should be easy because I do not have too many.

At the age of eighty-eight she had a cataract operation, and upon seeing me with her new eyesight, she showed surprise and said, "I never knew you had wrinkles on your neck."

I replied, "Mama, I'm not twenty anymore." She right away offered a solution. I should take better care of myself and use a hot oil pack at night and cucumber juice in the morning.

She gave me confidence in my appearance throughout my life. Whenever I went to a party she said I was the most beautiful, certainly the most elegant and charming girl or young woman. She still thinks I am younger looking than women my age, and if I am tired or neglect myself, she says it is because of her -- because she takes up a lot of my time, or because I underwent so many hardships that ruined my youth: the Holocaust, living in a communist regime, emigrating from Romania after waiting twelve years for a visa. She goes on and on explaining what I have experienced. Deep inside, though, I am sure she knows that her support all during those years, especially after Papa's death, was greater than any daughter could hope for.

This is why our bond is so strong that we think it can last forever. It is so unique that people cannot understand it, and they wonder why I suffer so inconsolably at the thought of her departure from this world. She has, after all, lived one hundred years. People are amazed that I would never separate from her, not even when I married, not even for a short time.

Rachel, you must see that you are fortunate to have such a good brother. I lost mine at the age of seventeen.

When my American uncles and aunts asked that I come to the United States and register in an American college, get married, become an American citizen and return to Romania to bring my mother to the U.S., I flatly refused. Who would take care of my Mama? It was not her financial well-being I worried about -- she was talented and hardworking. My concern was her emotional life. How could she go on alone after suffering the catastrophe of losing her entire family? We considered ourselves lucky to have each other. She was the only mother of millions who survived with her daughter. We simply could not separate.

When I was a child she gave most of her attention to my brother, who needed her, but I felt her love even without a lot of kissing and hugging. My affectionate nature comes from my father, who was very loving, and often hugged us with his long and strong arms. His warmth penetrated both my brother and me.

My mother was strict; she was always fair to my brother but not always to me. Sometimes she tried to explain why she seemed unfair to me but most of the time she left it up to me to understand her partiality to Zoltán. I think she felt badly when she could not give me all I asked of her. She worked hard to help solve my brother's eye problems, and it took much of her time and energy. She used to go to Cluj where there were famous doctors. She stayed with Zoltán during his surgeries and treatments, sometimes for weeks. Naturally, I felt cheated and abandoned. My father was miserable without her, but he tried to comfort me.

Recently, Mama and I talked about this time in our family's life together. She spoke of how unhappy she was when she returned home with my brother after eight weeks absence, and I, who was only five years old, ran from them and tried to pull my father away from them. I even cried when my mother tried to kiss me. I have not forgotten these feelings but I have never gone to therapy to cope with them. I feel that the closeness of our relationship in my adult life has cured everything and erased my small hurting memories.

Of course, Mama and I have had many arguments. Each of us is pretty strong in our opinions. Somehow, though, reconciliation has always been fast and easy. We forgive each other without concerning ourselves with who won the argument. Mama learned faster and adapted to changes with much more flexibility than I did.

It is a long way from our little village to Scarsdale, New York. She has reached the age of one hundred and one without faltering from the road. She has had her bad days, feeling down and pessimistic or having hopeless moments, but her common sense and love for life always overcomes any bitterness or temporary depression.

Now, after nearly two hours in the operating room, and one hour in the recovery room, my mother awakes and says, "You brought me back from the other world. Do I live now or do I dream?" She goes back to sleep.

Twenty minutes later, my friend Carol arrives to see her and support me. When Carol says to her, "I love you very much," Mama answers, "So do I," and sleeps again.

A long time passes before she asks for water. Only a few hours ago Dr. Siegler told me that he has done everything that is medically possible: he removed part of the tumor that choked the right kidney, but Mama has the kind of cancer that spreads quickly. The most important thing, he says, is that she should not suffer and there are many pain medications that can help her.

I cannot react or speak. When the tears come, I ask him how long will she live, and he replies that he does not know because he is not God.

He will evaluate her condition again in three months. I hope that she will live even three months more, so that I can have some more time with her. I feel strongly that we will have some time to talk, to relive and share remembrances of our past. I will be with her until the end comes.

It is eight o'clock at night. I have to leave the hospital, but the nurses don't chase me out. I help them to translate my mother's small requests in Hungarian. She asks me again if I have brought her back from the other world.

"I can't believe it," she says, "the scene is the same as after my gall bladder operation, my pacemaker, and now this, when I really died. Don't push," she says, "I'm old and only a burden for you -- let me go -- I am thanking God to be with you. We have had good times and bad times, but we have been together."

We say good night and she asks me to come early the next morning.

From July 7th until July 13th, Mama is in the hospital, and I spend most of each day there. She sends me home but waits for me to come back. She wants to live, but only if she can live well; she does not want to be a vegetable. She wants very much to be sent home where she knows I will take better care of her than these nurses who do not understand her.

"Let me die in my own bed," she says.

She falls asleep in the middle of conversations but we talk. Together we recall different periods of our lives, and she remembers details better than I do. She says that when she turned one hundred, she was reminded of her past, and that now is the time to tell it to Rachel and Robert. They are our family and they will be the link from our generation to the next. We must help them remember. We must tell them why George has only one grandmother, no grandfather, and has no first cousins, aunts, or uncles.

Mama is urging me to write about the family we lost in the Holocaust. She says her great-grandchildren must learn from our past and the legacy of our family history, our values, aims, sacrifices and shortcomings. Who will talk to them about these things if not me, the only survivor of the thirty-seven people?

She never learned English properly; there was no time for it. George spoke Hungarian because of Mama, but his knowledge of it is limited to that of a five-year old. He learned German in kindergarten, Romanian in preschool, French in first grade in Paris, and English in second grade at The Bronx School in New York.

Mama spent most of her time with George because Papa and I worked all our married lives. Papa worked in the chemical plant and moonlighted in pharmacies. Mama cooked and worked around Paul and George's schedules. I did not have any demands. If it was pasta, it had to be cooked half an hour before lunch or dinner, whatever Paul's schedule required.

George ate small, freshly cooked meals five times a day. Mama would go to the market early in the morning to get whatever vegetable was freshest and least expensive. She bought a hen that would lay an egg every other day for George's breakfast. He liked it soft-boiled on a slice of homemade bread. Even in 1956, ten years after the war, one could not always find fresh bread or good bread, so Mama baked it whenever she could. After the war, meats like beef and veal were rationed, but we could buy poultry from the market and take it to the *shohet* to be cut and made kosher, because Mama would not have it any other way.

In spite of her unfailing observance of our religious beliefs, when Paul would get pork chops from farmers, Mama would prepare them for him or for George without objecting, but she would not let me eat pork which I did -- but I did not dare to eat it in front of her. I had been hungry for too long in the concentration camps and had lived without meat for ten months, so I did not observe the kosher regulations outside of the house, but I tried not to hurt my mother's feelings. Before the war, though, Mama had a perfectly running kosher house.

My father followed Mama's leadership not only in the house, but in business as well. He liked his work and enjoyed talking to the customers, but the business-minded person was Mama, who talked to salesmen and selected the nicest ready-made shoes to be ordered for our store.

The manufacturing of shoes was my father's occupation, and my mother prepared the best possible meals for the man of the house and for his two children. She fed us all first, and whatever was left was hers. She ate the chicken head and the poultry feet (goose, duck, or chicken and sometimes the wings, which are still her favorite food).

She loves the fatty part and still eats it, disregarding her cholesterol intake.

I watch her now, helpless and "useless" as she puts it, and I cannot believe what has become of this active and strong woman. The weight loss reminds me of what I saw happen to her in the concentration camps when we dug trenches from September to January of 1945. I remember watching her then and seeing how thin she had become. A string held her coat closed, and it became double breasted, wrapping around from left to right, first four inches, then six and finally reaching around underneath her arm. My mother said this was okay because it kept her warmer.

Again, I see her get thinner every day; her beautiful skin is wrinkling, but her face is still pretty, though pale. She cannot walk out into the garden to enjoy the autumn leaves. She looks out of the window and wonders if she will ever be able to walk outside again, or if she will be able to once again climb the steps to her room where she would always watch the apple tree blooming, and the little apples forming and growing, until finally they would fall and decorate the lawn.

Mama enjoyed all these little pleasures; her demands in life were modest. She never had diamond rings, fur coats, crocodile pocketbooks, or expensive clothing. All she needed was a little attention and warmth from her family and a small group of friends. When I was a child, she never went on vacation, except for a few short five or six-day trips to see my grandparents.

My father had to take a number of trips for treatments at a bath resort for vascular problems in his leg, the result of too much standing. This occurred every two to three years, and my Mama would stay home and handle the house and the business. It was always in summer, so Zoltán and I were home and able to help: I with the cooking, Zoltán with the garden. Zoltán loved nature and enjoyed working in the garden. Mama did not feel the need for vacations as long as we were home.

I only saw her bitter and depressed two times in her life: once, when my brother had eye operations with unsuccessful outcomes and hopeless recoveries, and then when the Hungarians took the business and left her with no possibility of work or of us attending school.

Yesterday, I asked my mother what small moments made her happy. I want her to remember these things to lift her spirits now that she is suffering constant pain and fatigue. She remembered when I came home from school whistling an easy melody, bouncing up two steps at a time, cheeks rosy, filled with excitement, and told her, "Mama, I got a good mark in science!" And she remembered Zoltán, eyes covered from surgery, telling her with pride that he could multiply and divide numbers in seconds in his mind. When he told her this, she cried from happiness. She also recalled my father coming home from the open market, which took place every week in a different little village, reporting to her that he had sold all his merchandise, and had made enough money to start a new batch of shoes -- a full week's work.

At night we talk about our happy moments and little problems, and it feels so warm, like true contentment. She talks about the Friday night dinners, after which we would sometimes sit beside the six-foot tall tiled fireplace, feeling pleasantly tired and looking forward to the Sabbath -- a day without problems. She ends these recollections with a sigh and a question: "Will there be any more moments like those?" She dozes into a light sleep and I watch her and ask myself the same question.

I tell Mama that George might come for a couple of days to see her. At first her face lights up, but then she asks why he should see her in this condition. It would be better, she thinks, that he remembers her, as he always said, "A pretty old lady -- no one prettier."

"Now," she says, "I am really old and sick. What would he say if he saw me? Still," she says with her eyes shining, "it would be great to hug him once more."

The visit from George, though, was not so good. There was anxiety in the air. George tried to find a solution to ease my work for Mama. He wanted to get nurses around the clock and to minimize visits from my friends, and I saw my mother looking into the distance through me and far from George, slowly telling him by his Hungarian name, "Gyuri, I don't like strangers. I like friends and your mother needs friends. If I go, she is alone and her friends will comfort her."

George felt helpless and left earlier than planned.

Mama never understood or fully accepted why George's wife, Debbie, did not come for her one hundreth birthday -- which was celebrated across the whole country and abroad by other Holocaust survivors – or to her funeral, to be together with her husband, and you their son, Robert, and daughter, Rachel. She felt something was missing from our unity as a family. Respect for each other? Sharing joy or grief? Religious tradition or history? She could not find the reason but she was concerned about our future stability, spiritual and emotional, as a family. I could not help her understand, because I was puzzled myself, and George did not want to talk about it. George asked her to accept them as they are. Debbie is his wife and this is her decision.

Three months have elapsed since Mama's surgery, and Dr. Siegler wants to see her in his office to determine the position of the stent, because it can sometimes cause infection. We have to make a reservation for a special ambulette, because Mama can only take a few steps with the walker, which she hates passionately. It is October 15th, and she and I are both excited and afraid about the examination. I point out the trees in our garden -- the yellow, red, and burnt orange hues of autumn -- to distract her. She is quiet all along the road to Bronxville.

The examination is a simple sonogram and, thankfully, painless. The doctor is surprised, because her kidney looks much better than it did three months ago. He tells me to take Mama to the hospital in January, 2000 and he will change the stent.

"Doctor," I ask, "this means that she will live longer?"

He replies that she can live months, a year, or even years. He does not know for sure. If she has pain, he will increase the dosage of painkillers. The most important thing is that she should not suffer.

But Mama is very weak. She can hardly wait to get into her bed to rest. This time she is not joking, as she was the last time we visited the doctor in May, 1999. That time the doctor examined her and it hurt. I held her hand and it trembled as she yelled from the pain. The doctor finished his work then and left the office. I helped Mama dress, and she was very sad. I asked her if she still had pain and she said she did not but was sad for another reason. I asked why.

"Did you see how handsome Dr. Siegler is?" she asked.

"Yes," I answered, "but what is so sad about that? It is a good thing to be handsome!"

"But he was so close to me, all over me, and I did not feel any pleasure," she said. That she would say this at the age of one hundred and one really made me laugh at her humor and willingness to accept her age with resignation, and she smiled at me.

This time, however, she could not joke and she did not want to disappoint me in my hopes. The doctor does not know that she is weaker every day and that she has a hard time getting up every night; sometimes she must rise from her sleep five or six times to use the commode. He also does not know that her appetite is waning and that

I am constantly trying to give her nourishment by giving her some small amount of food of her choice.

Each night we discuss what she might like to eat the next day. For breakfast there is little choice, but she puts sugar in her coffee, which she can well afford now, because she has lost so much weight. She asks for a pear, cereal, and sometimes a slice of toast. Recently, I discovered that wheat-grass pills help her with her bowel movements. Each time she calls me I watch helplessly as she suffers, but she sends me away when she sees me so desperate.

I continue to teach at Eastchester High School three times a week, but I come home every free period. It takes me ten minutes to get home and I am able to see her, have lunch with her, and give her a painkiller. I talk a little about the school and the kids to distract her from her illness. She has visitors every day: Sandy, my neighbor, who loves and respects my Mama, and Carol, in spite of moving and selling her house, comes too and entertains her. She says that when she arrives Mama is sixty percent well, and when she leaves her, she is seventy-five percent well.

Company is always welcomed, but it is hard on her vanity. She cannot go more than one and a half to two hours without going to the bathroom. I look at her and beg her to get up or send the guest from her room, but she will not budge. She does not want to be seen struggling and bent pushing her walker. Louisa or I must stay behind her, ready to catch her if she loses her balance.

Once, a few weeks after her operation, she fell while leaning towards her chair, but nothing broke. She moved on. She complained for two or three days, but did not blame anyone, although there had been three people there.

That night when I gave her her prayer book and scarf, she told me quietly, "Klari, you want me to live, heal, and be with you long enough to be a burden on you, but God must hear me. I love you, but I destroy your comfortable life and your home because of all the changes you must make to keep near me all the time. You cannot rest; you cannot read or go out to a movie, concert, or bridge, without the agony of worrying about me. This has to end, no matter how hard it will be for you. That is the order of life. You gave me everything a child could give to her mother and much more. You will live without guilt forever, and you deserve a little happiness. I know you'll miss me, but you'll learn to handle your loss and you won't see me suffering. That will help. Only your father was as good as you and so unselfish with those he loved, but no one is as patient and warm as you are with me. Wait -- give me my painkiller. It's nine o'clock and I have gotten used to it. God bless you."

She turned on her left side and went to sleep.

I can't sleep. I listen to her breathing, listen for her movements. When she gets up, I see her struggle to reach the commode. She will never wet the bed. I go to her bedside and help her, and she looks at me and says, "You are here again. I did not call you. I did not ring the bell."

I say, "Now is the time to call me. Don't worry. I'll make up those couple of moments of sleep."

I don't know how relieved she is, but another Tylenol puts her to sleep for another hour or so. I have no hopes anymore, and just one wish: to lessen her pain. But I never wish to be without her.

The Rozsas, Papa's best friends, visit the next day. They stay more than two hours and Mama reminisces vividly. They say she looks better and more alert than ever, but when they leave at 9 p.m., she says she will say her prayers from memory. She has no energy to read. I tuck her into bed and wait until 10 p.m., when I give her her painkiller, and she falls asleep.

The days begin to go faster. She sleeps more, recuperating the hours of night sleep she loses. Her body, her strength, gives up. She talks about Thanksgiving. Maybe George and his family will come home, but she feels that if Debbie will not come again, the family should not come at all. Then she speaks about her funeral -- how simple it should be -- but she does not mean that her death will come so fast. It is most important, she says, to have a "minyan" -- ten men -- and she gives me the names I can count on: Gyuri Rozsa, Imre, Misi Sava his son, George, Radnoti, George Froyton (because he lives in Scarsdale it will not be asking too much of a sacrifice for him to come). She does not want to ask that anyone give up leisure time because of her. Of course, my George will be here, and then she stops.

Who else? I do not want to help her find anybody. I say she must live to find more men for the minyan. Then she is sad that all the relatives -- Moritz, Harry, and the others -- have died. They were always there for funerals, weddings, and bar mitzvahs. "Well," she says, "Harry Epstein and Zalmi will come."

It is Tuesday, November 2nd, and she wakes up tired after the third night of being diapered two to three times. This is most difficult for her to cope with; it offends her sense of dignity. When Louisa comes she is ready to be washed, but only very gently, because her body is so sensitive. She eats very little and promises she will make it up at lunch.

I leave reluctantly for school, but I have a very easy day, and spend most of it at home anyway. At 2:30 p.m. I come home again and Mama is asleep. She sleeps for two to three hours. When she awakes I am standing near her bed. She is so rested and content. I asked how she feels. She says she has never been better. Nothing hurts and it feels as though she could get up and walk again. She has come back from a different world, she says, a much better one. Her eyes are shining and her smile is happy. She quotes Papa, who said that if you wake up at the age of seventy and nothing hurts, you are dead.

"Klari," she asks, "am I dead? I ask because right now nothing hurts. Let me kiss you. You gave me life again."

It is unusual for my Mama to kiss me. She eats a little more for dinner, makes fun of my cooking a new discovery: milk soup with noodles followed by a hot dog with horseradish sauce. But pretty soon she is in pain again. At night we cannot control her pain and we are awake the whole night. I call Dr. Weber to ask what I should do, and she prescribes the first morphine pill for the night. This will give her twelve hours of sleep.

I stay home with Mama during the day and she takes more painkillers, but continues to suffer. I can see that she is weaker, yet at 9 p.m. she still fights when I give her the new painkiller. She says "Why take it? Today this pain would not stop."

Still, she relents and then sleeps more than twelve hours and does not react when I try to wake her. The doctor said she would sleep out the drug, but I can tell that she is not simply sleeping.

Imre and Louisa agree, and I call the ambulance. At the emergency room they do all kinds of testing, but only her heart is working -- even that may be only because of her pacemaker. They take her to intensive care and her condition does not change. She is in a coma. I talk to her constantly, but she does not react. Maybe she hears me. I think she opens her eyes, but this could be my imagination. I hope she hears me when I tell her how much I love her, and how I owe everything to her love, support, and care.

Imre stays with me until noon, goes to see his patients, and comes back. We stay in her room until midnight, a terrible hour when we are without hope. I am in touch with George in California who tells me, as do the nurses, that I should go home. The doctors come to see her, including a proctologist who cared for her a long time ago. He saw her name on the intensive care list. He tells me honestly that this is the end. He admired Mama when he treated her, and says that even now she is still fighting for her life.

Friday morning I call the hospital and the head nurse tells me that there is no great change, only her heartbeat is weaker, so I should come in. At 9 a.m. George calls and tells me that his grandma is gone. He called the hospital at 6 a.m. Pacific time, and received the news. When I arrive at the hospital, she is covered.

For the first time I feel that I am an orphan. My friend and companion of my whole life, my great mother, is gone. Does she know that she will always be in my heart, living and loved?

The proctologist sits with me and says, "Clara, you know what I loved in your Mama? Her name -- Pepi. This represented her. Look at her face. Even now she has a kind of curious smile. She is wondering where she is going and who will be there. People she loved? She is so curious." He makes me feel that he really knows Mama.

The nurses let me be alone with her until the funeral home officials arrive. For two hours I talk to her about our life and what we have gone through together. I ask again for forgiveness like I have on Yom Kippur every year of my life. She never accepted any apology, because she always said I had done nothing for which she should forgive me. Now she cannot answer and that hurts me.

Sunday is the funeral and your Dad comes alone. That hurts too, but Debbie has a serious reason for not coming, and of course, you won't come without her. Pepi does not know, and she would forgive you anyway. Your Dad eulogizes his Grandma and speaks beautifully. Carol reads a beautiful poem, and the Rabbi talks to my heart in understanding me. He says that the more one stays with a parent, the more attached one is, and the more difficult the departure. And this is why my grief is inconsolable; we were together too long, yet, I enjoyed every minute with her and I will miss even our quarrels.

At the cemetery, Carol, my Mama's great admirer and my friend, reads a poem she wrote to remember Mama. It makes me cry so hard that I can hardly control my sobbing. Then your father eulogizes his grandmother again, and my heart goes out to him. He had only one grandmother and never knew any other grandparents because they were killed in Nazi extermination camps, died in slave labor camps of malnutrition and illness, and fell from the frost in death marches. He does not have cousins, uncles, or aunts in Europe or America; only grandmother was close to him. She was always home when he returned from school, sports events, and outings with friends. She was the first to hear the news about good marks or disappointing ones. Whatever his successes or failures, she was there to listen. Mama saw the world through George, Paul, and me.

Your dad's eulogy is warm, revealing Mama's humor in situations that could be serious. He emphasizes Mama's intelligence, common sense, and ability to exercise it when others were losing control of theirs. His words touch me deeply. I see him trying to cope with his loss and trying to comfort me too.

He tells the story of his second ride in the car to our summer home. He and Mama drove on a Friday to the Swiss Forest near the lake where we spent the weekend. At the highway exit the car skidded and turned one hundred and eighty degrees back onto the road, facing the opposite way.

He stopped and looked at Mama to reassure her and calm her fears, but Mama only said calmly, "Gyurikam, I think we are on a wrong road. You want to return?" and smiled sheepishly.

George puts our friends at the funeral at ease in their sorrow. His words reveal his admiration for Mama and his sense that we must take consolation in the knowledge that we had a person like Mama in our lives and will continue to have her as long as we remember her in our hearts.

The sun is shining beautifully the day of my mother's funeral, but the wind is freezing and biting. After George's speech, I can only say a couple of words to thank everybody who has come to support us and who have been such good friends to Mama in all the years that have passed. They would bring her Romanian and Hungarian books, newspapers, recipes, jokes, and clippings so that she could satisfy her constant curiosity and be up-to-date with what was going on in the outside world. These people came to see her, to chat with her after their work, and whenever they had a few moments to spare. I can only feel gratitude towards them, for they contributed strongly to my mother's well being all these years. She must have been the only mother who survived the world wars and could project such love for life in spite of her sufferings. When she shared with them stories of the things she had seen and experienced in her life, they would learn how to better enjoy the little things in life and be contented by helping others in need.

She used to tell the story of a gentleman who wanted to marry her in America when we lived in Eastchester. He came two or three times a week to our house, and George and I once saw them holding hands. He was a pleasant man and loved my mother. One day he told Mama he hoped that when they married she would no longer help me so much all the time. Mama said that she would help as much as she could, because we were her family.

After this incident their relationship changed. Mama felt that he was selfish and that she would not leave us for anybody. Her upbringing taught her that a mother's priorities were family, children, husband, home, work, and friends -- in that order. Her faith and this philosophy helped her to maintain the everyday balance that we relied on throughout the journey of our small family.

Mama's picture at 100 years old

Chapter Twelve:
The Infamous Stutthof

n September 1944, we arrived in Stutthof, an important center for concentrating, selecting, and exterminating Jews, but we were not aware of this when we got there. On the surface it was neat and orderly: plants grew around the barracks.

Stutthof was a concentration camp for transient prisoners where we were deloused, disinfected, and selected for further work.

The shouting of SS men and women was by now familiar. It began with roll calls, where we stood for hours to be counted over and over again. Lunch was nowhere in sight, and when it did come, it was the same soup of salty grits and an occasional carrot. We were terribly hungry and tired.

One SS woman announced the "nachschlag" was on its way. "We have some extra soup. Stand on line and you'll get one more ladle. Come on youngsters. Die junge."

So everybody tried to get some more. I was the last to get on line. Mama was way up in the front. When the SS woman saw her, she slapped her so hard she lost her balance and yelled at Mama, "You old Fresser." (This meant that she ate a lot).

Of course Mama had gone to get the soup for me! There was no time for explanations and Mama's dear left cheek was burning from the pain, and her tears were flowing. I ran to her. She had been punished because of me. It hurts me even now as I write about it.

We disappeared from the sight of the SS woman. I hated her with all my heart, but did not want to make her happy seeing my suffering. The brutal satisfaction on her face was inhuman. She yelled at us that the leaders who ran the camp demanded order and discipline. We had better learn this because we would be there for two or three days before we were transferred to the work camps. We were to be herded to the shower room to be disinfected and deloused. Those who were found with lice were to be shaven again. We had to leave our clothes in the entrance hall because we would get clean, disinfected dresses. The SS woman barked this at us, then ended by shouting; "Los, austräten."

Finally, we came to the room where we washed ourselves.

It was so controlled in the washrooms that they made us scrub even the inside of our shoes with disinfectant. My boyfriend Ervin's picture faded so badly that I could no longer recognize his face. His photograph was my last connection with my past. I mourned its loss for a long time.

They made us stand on line, wet and itching from the chlorine-filled water, waiting for clean clothing. You should have seen what was thrown to us: ripped and ruffled, but disinfected from the last week's transport group. I received a green satin cocktail dress fitted for a size six. Although I had lost a lot of weight, I was still a size eight or ten, so I had to open the seams to be able to wear it. I also had a pair of panties and full-slip in which I slept. It was ridiculous to think that these were my only clothes for five months of digging trenches, repairing shoes and cutting trees in the forest.

Mama again got a coat-dress, long and colored beige, and I thought immediately that from her dress I could cut off enough if I still got my period. She also had a black cotton slip and panties. We only had lice in our clothing in Kaiserwald, and not too many. We killed them the minute we noticed them. We heard the girls crying who were shaved again when the SS woman saw even a lice egg in their hair.

I can see your faces, Rachael and Robert, how much pity and disgust you must show reading about our situation in the new camps. I wanted to write about what we went through, simply because we were Jewish. Religious or not, we have not been accepted for thousands of years. Because of our laws of the Torah and belief in one God, we were always different and often hated. The Nazis hated us the most; their purpose was to annihilate all the Jews in the most painful ways: humiliation, degradation, and torture until the final solution: gassing us when we are no longer any use to them.

Our barracks was not far from the washing room, so we hoped we'd have more chances to bathe, but we were told that we wouldn't stay long in Stutthof. There was no work for us here, so we waited. Meanwhile, we met other Hungarian groups. To my happiness, there was Blimu, Ervin's sister, who was my friend, my classmate, and with whom I could talk endlessly about Ervin. She loved her brother and so did I. We had to catch up on so many incredible events. There were people, mutual friends, and family to talk about. We made plans for the future and tried to stay together, though we didn't know whose group would be better, and what risks we would take in our new situations.

Blimu wanted to come with us no matter where, because of Mama. She was with two girls from our town, but they were not friends. She considered me as her future sister-in-law; Ervin had told her about our plan to marry after the war. Blimu was spoiled as the only daughter in her family. Ervin and Arthur were her older brothers. She was intelligent, but could not adjust in these situations, as I had. She was passive, and let things happen without fighting for survival. Everyone said how she revived with us in those three days at Stutthof.

The first night we tried to smuggle Blimu into our barracks, but we had a roll call and the SS woman recognized from the number on her dress that she belonged to another barracks.

Blimu and I spent nearly three hours in each other's barracks. We became close friends. We used to be friends before, but in the time right before we left our village she had begun to resent that Ervin was so attached to me that he spent more time with me than with his family. He would spend all the time until curfew in my house and then he would go home for dinner and sleep.

Once we met in Stutthof, however, and we talked about the past, Blimu said that she understood how much her brother loved me and how he knew that what was happening could mean the end of his dream of marrying me. Blimu hoped, of course, that somehow after the war we would all be together as we were before. We did not say goodbye that night, and the next day we were transported from Stutthof. I never saw her again. Another survivor told me that Blimu died of diphtheria in another camp.

There was no way we could keep her with us. The next day, Blimu met Magda, her neighbor from our town, in her barracks and she took her under her protection although she was, herself, very weak. Magda was older, twenty-eight years old, and could protect her. I did not give up trying to save her, however, and asked our supervisor, the Kapo, if she could help us stay together. She promised she would try but did not succeed.

The third day our group was ordered to pack up, form our lines, get our ration of bread and lard, and walk to the train station. The train station! It was about three miles from the camp, and when we saw the train we couldn't believe that it was for us. Regular third passenger cars with wooden benches we hadn't seen before! There were toilets between the cars and a mirror above the sink!

Oh God! When I saw my face, my one-inch uncombed hair, my yellow teeth, and my low-cut satin dress, I started to laugh hysterically. How come my Mama hadn't said anything to me about my looks? On the other hand, why would she? She couldn't help me change my appearance anyway.

Poor Mama, how miserable she must have felt when she saw me coming to her bench. Even now she looked decent in her long, double-breasted dress of nineteenth century fashion. The first of September was quite warm for this long-sleeved dress, but she felt more comfortable than I did in my ridiculous outfit. She helped me overcome my low confidence with her sense of humor; "Dearest, think of going to a five o'clock tea party where you will attract all the attention with your avant-garde fashion. Your high-ankle shoes, unfortunately, cover your beautiful ankles, and the dress covers your knees. Still, your legs are showing, but the rest is really modern and probably up to date. You are pretty anyway."

I wanted to believe her, so I didn't look at myself in the mirror anymore.

Chapter Thirteen:
New Horizons - Dorbeck

The train put all of us in a better mood. After all, this wasn't a cattle wagon or a cargo ship. When the SS men stepped out we even sang old songs to the rhythm of the train: Hungarian, Romanian, and even the *Ode to Joy* by Beethoven — in German. We were young, and any little sparkle of light could invigorate us. Mama was listening, but did not sing along; not because she did not think she could hold a tune, but because she was thinking of something more important: the high holidays were approaching and our family was nowhere to be seen.

There was no hope of being freed to go home. Who knows where our husbands, sons, mothers, brothers, or families were? We had no idea if they were even alive or not. The train rode on without stopping for two hours before slowing down in front of a small station -- Dorbeck. It seemed as though we were in the middle of nowhere when we descended, but in the far distance we could see small houses with red tiled roofs, and we knew it would be a long walk.

The SS men directed us in the opposite direction of the houses, toward the open fields. There was no horizon in sight. We marched and marched, silent and tired; the sun was on our backs, but it still warm, even though it must have been four or five o'clock. That was a very long day.

Where will we stop? Where will we sleep? Never mind the food. We are exhausted.

We saw one house far away that appeared in the middle of the wasteland. We found out later that was where our SS men would live. When we had gotten out of the train —one thousand women -- there were exactly twenty armed SS men and no SS women with us. Leon talked about running away — but where? "They won't kill us," she said, "They must have their slaves." She had this obsession to escape somehow.

The house grew bigger in front of us and the distance became smaller. The sun was ready to set behind us. We stopped one hundred feet from the building and were ordered sit on the dry dirt near some grass. We were told to wait for our dinner and for materials for tents, which we had to pitch if we wanted to sleep in them, or if not, in the open air. This would be like camping in Transylvanian summer camps, or so we thought.

That night we had warm grit soup and a slice of bread almost one inch thick -- not that it satisfied our hunger, but we hoped this would be our new ration. We built our tent for ten girls and some of us were really handy. When the straw arrived, carried by the farmer's cart with a horse, we realized this tent would be our home for days or weeks, even months, and it was not fun anymore. We slept on one blanket, and used another to cover us. This blanket later served me as a coat when winter came. We slept in our slips and panties like sardines in a box; our dresses served as our pillows. Our shoes were on the side of the tent. If one of us turned, the nine others had to turn too, like spoons in a neat kitchen drawer. We spent a restless night followed by many other nights until some time in October. We were so tired we almost always slept like logs.

When the sun rose, we were chased from the tent to wash. Near the SS's building there were three or four faucets above a sink which was used to feed animals. Just imagine how many girls washed that day, embarrassed at being in front of the men who were watching?

We heard the heard the orders: "Kaffe holen!" (Bring the coffee.)

Then another: "Stand on line! Wait for breakfast!"

Breakfast was warm liquid bran, with saccharin, and coffee -- another brown liquid with saccharin, that had very little coffee in it. It had no taste, but it was something to drink. Then one slice of so called bread -- I never knew what it was made of, some kind of greenish-yellowish vegetable, not wheat, and with salt, though it never satisfied our hunger.

First we ate the cereal, then the coffee in the same dish with the bread. We ate every crumb, slowing down near the end of the meal so it could last longer. We watched each other, seeing who could make their bread last the longest. Babuci ate so slowly that everybody envied her, and she still had food when we were hungry again.

Food was our center of life; it had become so important that we sometimes couldn't think of anything else.

Leon was the only one who thought of trying to escape or of going on a hunger strike -- which was ridiculous in our circumstances, no one would join her. No one wanted to commit suicide; we wanted to get our revenge if we survived.

The sunrise made the day bright.

It was maybe 7 a.m. when we started our new assignment. We picked up shovels, axes, and spades, and began marching five kilometers to the fields where we dug anti-tank ditches, and other obstacles. The Red Army tanks and the Russians were supposed to fall into the traps that we dug for twelve hours daily until sunset, and soon the East-Russian borders were supposed to be crisscrossed by our defensive tank traps.

There were different kinds of trenches in Dorbeck. We dug one kind one yard wide and two yards deep which spanned in length, zigzagging for kilometers without any break. Every morning we found the territory pre-marked by engineers we never saw; we had only seen some guards and young boys, my age or younger, who had watched us working. They were our slave drivers; who yelled at us if we stopped, or relaxed a minute or just slowed down.

In the beginning we preferred this work, outside in the open air. In September and October it was refreshing after all of our night-shifts in the factories of Riga. I learned how to use a spade, how to make steps on the side of the ditch to get about seven feet deep, and how to throw the dirt to the right-hand side where my mother and another girl shoveled and smoothed the soil, leveling it with the field. In the ditch there was another girl who was doing the left side, throwing the dirt to two girls in the same way I was on my right. The two of us worked fast with the spade, but we could rest when the ditch was at the deepest point, for nobody could see us. It was hard work, and after two or three weeks we were thinking longingly about the factory where we used only our hands, instead of our whole bodies.

At midday, we came up to eat our meager lunch of bread and coffee. Sometimes they gave us marmalade, and very rarely, a kind of knockwurst made of horsemeat, which my mother didn't eat. That September there wasn't too much rain, but October made up for it. Our midday meals were wet, and we would try to get into the ditch, and cover our heads like a tent with our blankets. Then the blankets would be wet at night and we couldn't use them as our covers.

After the ten minute meal break, we would run around for spots to empty our bladders -- another torture. Now that I describe this, it seems impossible how we did it without any paper, rag, or anything to clean us with, only green leaves. Sometimes we wanted to find a green spot with leaves, but there was no time to waste with this necessity. We had to save some coffee for our return to wash our fingers.

The dirt from the ditch was always wet. The groundwater was yellow from clay and mud. *Can you picture this, Rachel?* But when the sun came out from behind the clouds, we dried and warmed up by working. We talked, sang, and recited poems to forget our misery. Meanwhile, Babuci's and my Mama exchanged food recipes which they had cooked or baked from at home a long time ago. This drove us crazy. We couldn't think of those foods because we were so hungry. Mama and Babuci's mother prayed almost constantly.

If we were too loud, the Hitler-Jugend, the young punks, yelled at us, called the SS, and they would scream, "Was quatsched ihr (what do you blab about)?"

Then there was silence, and the work had to go on, and fast.

The afternoons were longer. We worked until sunset, 6 or 7 o'clock. When we returned to our tents, we passed by fields and smelled the ripe turnips -- that was the best food for animals. In the morning, we didn't even try to step out of the line and steal one, but when it was dark we ran out, hoping that the SS man would not see us. We succeeded two or three times, but once, when one girl was caught, the SS shot in the air, scaring us. It became too risky. They would kill us for stealing. They needed us for the trenches to trap the Russian tanks, but they would not allow us to steal cattle food.

Dinner was always the same: soup made of potato peels, some carrots, and starch. It was thick and filled us while we were eating. Sometimes we even got seconds if there were sick people who couldn't eat. More and more people got diarrhea, and could only drink water. There were no medicines, herbs or teas. Later there was some aspirin, we heard, but we never saw any.

One day in October my mother became very weak and couldn't move her right arm. I was concerned and went to the doctor of our camp. Dr. Kardos was a dentist in our town who had become a doctor for one thousand women, and she was arrogant and bitter. I asked her to let Mama stay home for half a day because she wasn't well, but she yelled at me, "I can allow one percent of the women to stay in. The rest should drop dead [but they have to go to work]."

Mama couldn't stay in the tent, so she soaked her fingers in hot coffee every morning so that she could move them. She developed arthritis. I hated that doctor! I'll talk more about of her crimes later, but I will tell you that, after our return to Cluj, Dr. Kardos was imprisoned.

The high holidays were at the end of September. How did Mama and Babuci's mother figure this out without a calendar? I don't know, but they prayed at night and two days at Rosh-Hashana, and in the morning during work in the trench. We remembered the clothing we had received for the New Year, the food we used to eat, and the honey in which we dipped our challah, so our life would be sweet the whole year. There was no Jewish family so poor that could not afford the best feast on these holidays. Fruit was always in abundance, wine was on every table for the Kiddush (prayer for the wine), and white starched tablecloths and candles lit up everybody's shiny face.

Many of us were angry with God who had let us suffer like this for no reason, or who maybe even didn't know about us. We didn't pray, and turned away from those who did, but I respected my mother too much to discuss my rebellious feelings, and I covered for her when she stopped working and prayed.

Chapter Fourteen:
Guttau – Lesson to a Hitler-Jugend

Between Rosh Hashana and Yom Kippur we got orders to pack up our belongings from our tents. We marched many miles to a place called Guttau in East Prussia. Here we moved into big, new, prefabricated tents made from wood panels in a hexagon shape made for one hundred people. They weren't quite finished when we moved in, but we carried in straw that was brought by trucks. The tent was double-decked with an entrance door. Its roof was almost flat and the rain came easily off the bottom of the big tent.

We dug trenches around the new tent so we wouldn't have groundwater under our beds, and our group continued to live together. We were only fifty people, because our Kapo, with her two sisters, had the privilege of having a box to themselves so they could store bread and some food, like the marmalade or margarine to be distributed in the morning -- at least that was the excuse for them to live better than the rest of us. They used our shares of margarine -- not to eat -- but for their faces, and didn't go out to work in the trenches. Instead, they reported to SS men, distributed food and during the day they helped in the kitchen.

The oldest of the three sisters, Aranka, lives now somewhere in Westchester, but I haven't tried to meet her. She was tall, stout, and had a pretty face that radiated among all the sad, overworked, drawn faces of the others. She had a white cotton scarf to cover her shaved head; it was starched with something that looked like a nurse's bonnet. I don't know where she got it. Her queen-like posture suggested authority, and most of us were scared when she gave her orders. Her big right hand moved fast and heavily when she slapped the girls for not obeying quickly. Her slogan was, "Do you want me to report you to the SS? That would be worse."

Even her sisters were afraid of her. Susie, her oldest, complained to me. I met her in 1983 at a gathering of survivors in the lobby of our hotel in Washington. She didn't recognize me, she said. Of course, we were only a mass of a thousand women and they were field leaders, fully subservient to the SS.

Mama asked me then, "Did you spit on her and call her a collaborator?"

"No," I said, "but I told her I didn't want to see her or her sisters ever again.

Susie understood, and said that Marta, her younger sister, died after the liberation by overeating fats and sweets before returning to their home. I felt sorry for her. She was the nicest of the sisters; she sometimes even stole bread from their supply and gave it to the hungry.

During our evacuation on January 19, 1945, we found about thirty whole loaves of bread – three hundred individual rations -- under their straw. They had slept on them. We knew that our rations had always been very small, but Aranka and her sisters made fourteen portions instead of ten out of the bread, so that they accumulated so much extra. But their bread had become covered in mildew so now it could not be eaten by anybody. Even our own leaders had cheated us and made our lives worse instead of better. I hope the girls who came from their town punished her. In my opinion only those who knew the circumstances in which we lived should have the right to judge others in the camps.

We were still working in trenches but this time we had a much more difficult task. The anti-tank ditches were now much larger (six yards wide and seven feet deep) and were shaped like trapezes, narrowing to one yard at the bottom. You will see it traced on the attached picture that was taken in 1995, fifty years later, by the brother of a man I met through an article about Mama when she turned one hundred years old. The brother visited the site to search for the mass grave where their sister was buried.

She had died there after our evacuation of the camps. About sixty corpses were left in a tent. We couldn't bury them because of the frozen ground. This tent was empty after the epidemic of paratyphoid and some hundred people died, most in December, 1944. Les told me that his sister died after we left the camp. She stayed with a friend who was so sick she couldn't walk. His sister nurtured her and tried to feed her, but her friend never recovered and died soon afterward. Les' sister caught her friend's disease. She sacrificed her life for her friend. After many years, the population of the village erected a monument with the numbers of some of those buried in the mass grave. The names of those buried were not known, only the numbers tattooed into their skin.

I never gave up my wish to go back to this place and to Riga, Dorbeck, and Guttau where I lost so many dear friends, but when I was at Auschwitz in 1994, fifty years later, I couldn't go there because the other tourists didn't care and didn't want to join me. I was the only survivor of the twenty-one people in the group; the other American and Canadian tourists were looking for their "roots" in Warsaw, Prague, and Vienna -- cities which had turned their ancestors over to the Nazis.

Maybe, Rachel and you, Robert, will come with me to see those places. Alone, it would be difficult for me to face those memories.

As you look at these trenches in the picture, you can see that even after fifty years, the widths and lengths did not disappear. The snow and the rain have not washed off the marked lines and have not completely filled up the hundreds of kilometers of excavation. Those houses in the distance were dorms for the SS guards. When they ran away later, partisans moved in and fought with the Russian army against those Nazis who tried desperately to fight back. Those trenches are proof of our incredible hard work for months in the heat, rain, and snow, where hundreds of human beings lost their lives.

At the end of October the cold weather set in, and by 6 p.m. it was dark. The guards chased us out of the tent early in the morning while it was still dark so we could get to work at the trenches by sunrise. The Russians were close by and we could hear the cannons during the night. We knew that the war was coming to an end, but did not know if we would live long enough to see it. We had no newspapers, radio, or contact with other human beings.

The young men, Hitler-Jugends, who supervised our work, sometimes dropped newspaper articles in our ditches, in which their lunch was wrapped. If we could read the stained paper, we read it avidly. The Germans still wrote nothing about the possibility of losing the war. Lies, lies! And we knew this though from their wild pushing to finish the anti-tank trenches. Nobody washed in the morning anymore, and we only had coffee and a piece of bread. There was no time to eat warm 'cereal' -- the bran-liquid.

Every minute it was important to be ready with "the great obstacle," as they called them -- the trenches that the Nazis expected would trap the Russian tanks. My spade was heavy, and shoveling out the wet dirt from the rain made it even heavier. I had to make steps on the side of the trench, like a ladder, so I could climb up from the bottom, and at the end I removed the steps one by one, and I smoothed the wall straight. It had to be perfect, or we were yelled at, beaten up, and not given dinner after we finished our six kilometer walk to the tent.

At night, the guards didn't care if we were slow, or if we were hungry or tired. We became more and more apathetic when we dragged ourselves home, stood in line for dinner, ate, and then dropped onto our bunks like logs. We would often wake up shortly afterwards because of the lice in our dresses and under our arms. The lice felt our warmth and slowly sipped our blood. We had to kill them and destroy their eggs every night and try to wash ourselves in the cold water of the river, through the darkness which was three hundred yards from the tent.

If we washed our clothes, one of us had to stay naked under the blanket. I usually did because Mama washed my dress and then some of her clothes. I washed the next day when my clothes dried during the night -- if they did. If not, I had to wear them damp.

Early frost in November really scared us. We thought we would not last the winter under these circumstances. Our lives in camp became unbearable, and more and more women had to stay in with paratyphoid fever. Our clothing was never meant for cold weather, and our shoes were worn out.

One day in the beginning of November, Mama felt weak, but she didn't dare stay in the camp. We knew that fresh air would help her more than staying in the tent with the sick people, so we marched to the fields to finish up the last piece of the trench where we had already worked for three days.

I went down to eliminate the steps from the side, and Mama shoveled neatly on top. It was around mid-day when I heard the young Nazi who supervised our work yelling at my mother to work faster, not like a "louse". When I heard his stick hitting Mama, I jumped out of my trench without thinking that I could be killed. I only thought that I had to protect her. I faced him within twenty seconds and confronted him full with my anger.

"Stop it!" I shouted. "Don't hit my mother."

He continued to yell, "You old bag, move faster." I came closer and we were face to face.

He stopped.

"This woman works twelve hours a day with the terrible food you give us, in rain, in frost, in the same clothing that she wears every day for four months. And you hit her? Don't you have a mother?"

With tears in my eyes I tried to control my anger. To everybody's surprise, he stopped, flabbergasted, red, and speechless.

Then he pulled himself together and answered. "Yes I have a mother, but she is German, not a Jew." Then he turned around and left without a word. All the girls thought he left to bring the SS man and take me who knows where. But nothing happened that day.

We all worked full of fear the whole afternoon. Mama was crying. What had I done? How could I have rebelled? He wouldn't have hit her forever, and I risked my life with my temper, and Mama tried to calm everybody by saying maybe this boy just will forget it.

I didn't sleep the whole night; I looked at my mother's back where I could see the mark of the stick of this thug who was my age or younger. How could I have kept quiet and let him get away with this? No, I didn't regret my interfering, even if I would be punished.

The next day we continued to enlarge the new ditch, and everyone in our group was worried what was going to happen. Sometimes they punished the whole group if one of us didn't complete the work she was expected to do. I knew my group would blame me if this incident punished them, but my friend Leon agreed with me that she would have done the same thing if someone hurt her mother.

Nothing happened until noon, when suddenly the boy appeared and came straight to our ditch. My whole body was trembling, but I didn't move or look at Mama.

The boy had a carrot in his hand and pointed it at me. "Eat this," he said. "It has vitamins in it." Then he gave me half of a cigarette and said, "Smoke it. You will be less hungry."

To my astonishment I said "Danke." That's all I could utter. He turned around and left without a word. We never saw him again.

I couldn't believe my eyes. I hugged Mama and cried. My heart felt like a stone, but my normal heartbeat returned. It seemed that I had reached this boy somewhere in his soul that had not been brainwashed by Nazi ideology. I had found some human feeling that was buried under his distorted education. I hoped that somewhere in each heart of every human being there could be good place ready to help if they could only see the right from wrong.

To the future generation: Don't give up on human beings especially when they are young. They can change evil into goodness. If you cannot do it alone, get a friend or friends to help you in your battle for a better society.

We were scared, frightened and most of the time, our thoughts were numb. Our thinking and actions depended on our physical condition: how hungry we were that day, how much water we had, if we were too hot or cold, or if we would be able to wash at night, or if we would have to suffer from filth, sickness, and lice through another sleepless night.

Yesterday I saw on Broadway the play *Judgment at Nuremberg,* the international trial of the SS judges after the war in Nuremberg. It brought up every detail in my memory of our misery between 1944 and 1945 in my little town where all the laws against Jews were enacted at the rise of Hitler. The leaders, the executioners of those laws were tried by an international court of judges, open to the public. The prosecutors called witnesses and presented films. Emotions took over when I heard the names of the twenty-five defendants, their functions, and their unanimous answers to the charges: "Not guilty for crimes against humanity/"

My dear friend Carol sat next to me in the theater, held my hand, dried my tears, and tried to comfort me in silence with her touch. She had also been with me when I saw *Schindler's List*. She comforted me when the scene of the selection in Auschwitz reminded me of my separation from my father, brother, and all my family that I never saw again. When Carol led me out from the movie, I was devastated by the images of that night, and felt the loss of my family just as painfully as I had fifty years before.

Rachel and Robert, I was so lucky that she was at my side with her compassion for a friend's suffering. Hearing Carol's kind words and soft warm voice, I came slowly back to reality as she drove me home to my dear Mama, your Great-grandma Pepi, who also was grateful to Carol and told her, "My daughter has a lot to live for -- her son and his family support her as she fulfills her mission to teach the world, 'Never Again.' And her grandchildren love her..."

She went on and on, until I told her that I was all right; I had just been overwhelmed with memories.

Carol was always with me and Mama with her understanding, warmth and consolation, and it was so sad when she moved so far away from Scarsdale,

Her closeness has been, and is the greatest help for Mama and for me over the last ten years, and her friendship is one of the most valuable assets in our lives. The world would be much better if there were more people like her. Her daughter once told me "My mother is a saint. She doesn't have a bad thought in her mind about anybody until it is proven that somebody is nasty, mean, or unethical. Then she distances herself from their company, but she would not hurt anybody."

The circumference line of an antitank trench after 50 years

Monument in Guttau

Chapter Fifteen:
Shoe Repairers Born

Cold set in early that year in Guttau, East Prussia. The first frost was in October; then snow fell in the beginning of November. It was so hard to dig the trenches that they used dynamite to start the digging and then we had to shovel the ground to the top of the ditch.

One Sunday when we stood for the morning roll-call there was an unusual announcement. A big bag of leather packaging and pieces of sole and rubber arrived in the camp for the mending and repair of the shoes of us prisoner-slaves. Our shoes were in such terrible condition that no one could go out to work if they were not repaired. Some women were given wooden shoes but they were impossible to wear in deep snow as it stuck to the shoe -- and walking fast was treacherous.

They needed shoe makers to repair the shoes. In Europe no women worked in this job, but the SS men didn't know this or didn't care. When I heard this, a quick thought rushed to my head. This work must be done inside. My father was a shoemaker and I would be able to do some things, mother even more, and perhaps with this work we could survive. I raised my hand and Mama looked at me, her eyes full of fear and incredibility. I pulled on her hand with my own left, and raised her arm. She was speechless but my quick thinking probably saved our lives.

The two of us were ready to repair shoes, I said. Not two minutes later, to our surprise, two other girls raised their hands. The four of us were then selected to inspect the materials and the tools that we would be used. This was my moment to prove to the SS man that we could repair shoes if he gave us a chance. I even began to imagine that we might even have heat from a small stove if we could cut branches in the forest to burn in it. This is what the SS promised us and we wanted to believe it.

The SS man asked some questions such as where did we learn this, and we said my father taught us. He was the best in our village; there were only two other shoe makers, and of course my father was the best. We even had witnesses, I told him. Mama couldn't utter a word, she was so shook up. I looked at the leather sole pieces and I remembered that these were like the pieces that we threw into our garbage. My father would never use them: they were too small to cover the holes. They were unusable even for a poor man, because the water would leak into the shoes, and the work would be worthless.

Now there was not even time to think to remember to cry about those memories. We had to live. Mama kept looking at me, her eyes asking me, "How can we help not just ourselves but our camp mates?" I whispered, "Mama, anything will be better than the shoes they are wearing. If we can mend shoes for one week, we can spare some of our camp comrades from cold and suffering."

So the SS gave us leather, needles, small nails and the bag of sole remnants that were thrown away by some shoemaker in Poland, and the four of us walked out with the treasure that would hopefully save our lives, or at the least, give us some more time.

Elizabeth asked the SS man to allow us to work in her tent where there was room in one cubicle from which two bunks had been removed. Ten people, it seemed, had died so that we could have space enough to repair the shoes. There was another half of a bunk where we could store the shoes to be repaired and also the ones we had repaired. One day everybody would happily pick up their "new" shoes and get rid of their wooden ones.

We were jumping up and down because we were settled in our great new job, but there were four or five very sick people who couldn't move and they stayed in the tent. They were hoping that we would give them some hot coffee or hot water from the kitchen when very few guards were around during the day. For me, this presented the possibility of not only helping them, but also letting me get out! I would run up to the kitchen two or three times a day for those poor people who were so dehydrated from constant diarrhea. Now we know they had paratyphoid fever.

They were so grateful for every drop of water. We didn't even know if their illness was contagious or not. We carried the water in our dishes and poured it in theirs. By the third week I had gotten familiar with the routine of the kitchen staff --three women who cooked for one thousand women in the beginning, then later, in November, only for the five hundred of us who were left. They worked very hard, but of course we envied them because, they had more potatoes in their soup, which was the only meal they prepared for us. They didn't peel the potatoes or the carrots, although we seldom had any. Otherwise, the kitchen staff thickened it with grits or starch -- something that filled us up for an hour.

One morning I went up for coffee and saw three potatoes near the big cooking dish. I picked them up and placed them under the dish while the wood burned. No one saw me. On my second trip I took them out. They were burnt, but still had something to eat in it. The burnt parts were eaten by the sick people who told us that it would clean their intestines like coal. Erika knew this to be true, since she was a pharmacist's daughter. Unfortunately, one of the girls died two weeks later, but I don't think it was from the coal.

Every week we had more and more corpses that we had to bury; twenty to fifty a week. The days were growing shorter and those girls who came from work were so tired that we could only bury once a week and then we could only dig one grave for all the bodies. Before we buried them, we took their blankets, shoes, and any warm clothing, and gave it to those who worked in the trenches.

We became numb -- both emotionally and physically -- from cold and hunger. We couldn't feel the tragedy anymore of how low we sank in "civilization" -- this morbid civilization.

Alice and Ellen lost their beautiful sister, Potyi. They couldn't wear their sister's blanket or clothes, so they gave them to me. It really helped in the death march later from January 19th to 21st. Alice lives now in Sydney, Australia. When we meet at our rare reunions, I think of her sister's blanket and how it saved me from freezing in the unusually cold winter.

My friends were happy for our special situation. Mother and I stayed together in a tent, and we knew that deep in their hearts they envied us. I don't blame them a bit. Lucu, Irene, Babuci, Eva -- they didn't even talk to me when we stood in line for our meals. But when the word spread that we were doing a good job repairing ten or more pairs of shoes a day, many of them became grateful.

We also repaired shoes with nails in them -- which was not so great, although they were easier to work with. Many times the nails wounded their feet, so we would have to sew them; but thread wore out faster, and they still had to be careful with the nails. When we used up all the sole pieces and leather, we cut up the usable old shoes and we used their good parts to repair the shoes we could save.

In one of these shoes Mama found two gold coins that she saved for who knows why, but after our liberation in Lublin, she was lucky to have them to spend. After the liberation, I was terribly sick, running a high fever. No doctor was around in the middle of nowhere. Mama was so desperate for help that she left me on a mattress on the floor with three other girls who couldn't get up because they were so tired after walking twenty kilometers. With no knowledge of the local language, she walked into the first small wartime pharmacy and started to speak Yiddish to the pharmacist and showed him one of those coins. A shabby Polish Jew came up to her and responded in Yiddish. He bought the coin from Mama and helped her buy the medicine for her sick daughter.

The pharmacist didn't understand anything about this transaction, but half an hour later he sold Mama some aspirin and tea while the shabby guy explained Mama's request. Mama was the first woman Auschwitz survivor seen by these men in Lublin. Here is further proof to show my grandchildren the role that fate played in our survival. The shoes of the prisoner who died in Guttau a long time before had saved two people and the prisoner whose shoes we mended saved my life five months later.

We were efficient and everyday we gained more experience working on those shoes. Our fingers were frozen sometimes, but the hot coffee or hot water from the kitchen helped to warm them up. One afternoon the old

SS guard surprised us by appearing in our tent door. He saw the sick women wrapped in their blankets shaking, and saw us working with the needles warming up our fingers in our mouth. He asked how we could work like this? He was a Nazi, of course, although we soon called him "Old Papa" in Hungarian, because he was kind to us when the other Nazis weren't around. He made a big difference in our lives because the next day, eight little iron ovens arrived in our camp.

We were given orders to place one in each wooden tent. We were also given some saws and permission to cut branches in the forest near the river to heat the tents at night when the women come home from the work. These little round iron ovens had to be constantly fed by coal or wood in order to give heat. Elizabeth's tent was the warmest, for we heated it during the day as well. The minute we didn't put wood in it, it cooled off in half an hour.

Our oven also served to dry our clothes when we could wash them once in a while. Only four people at a time could get near to it, so they wouldn't take away the heat from those who were sleeping in their bunks.

In 1994 when I visited Theresienstadt concentration camp near Prague, I saw an oven just like ours in a museum in Guttau. This view had such an impact on me that the tourist group I was with, thought I was going crazy. It brought back my memories of Guttau with its terrible conditions.

Two tents were empty by this time and they were used to isolate the very sick, dying women from the rest, and from the corpses that could be buried only once a week. (See the pictures of the trenches).

But we still existed! At night we went to the forest and cut branches. I was good at it and seemed to instinctively know how to use the hammer and saw.

At the end of November the puddles in the forest were frozen. We stood on them like they were skating rinks as we cut the trees. One time I didn't notice that the ice had broken and that my right foot was deep into the ice-cold water. I continued to work until I had cut enough wood for both the night and next morning. I had trouble getting my frozen foot out, but with help, I finally did and walked away from the puddle carrying my precious wood.

There were four other girls with whom we exchanged our tools. There were very few of us because the camp was not equipped for cutting wood in the winter for freezing slave laborers. The girls helped me get out of the ice and walk to my tent. Mama was very worried about my right foot. She struggled to pull off my shoes that were filled with the icy rags we had stuffed them with to keep me warm. I couldn't walk for hours. She found out forty years later that these injuries caused juvenile osteoarthritis. I also had a fever every day for a year after my liberation which was caused by untreated pneumonia. To this day I have the shadows of scars on my right lung.

That night in the tent my foot stayed numb for a couple of hours until the blood circulation slowly returned. Two of my toes even now become numb in winter and itch until they warm up. These minor problems are enough to remind me of my great mother and our misery in the slave labor camp.

The next day I could not put on my shoes and Mama went alone to the other tent to bring me some damaged shoes to work on in my bunk. It was cold, but during the day we were no longer allowed to make a fire in the tent. Everybody was out in the fields digging trenches. The very sick had their empty bunks in the two tents that had been occupied by those who died the month before.

Without our work, ten to twelve people would go barefoot everyday. We most likely saved lives by our work. Mama had to tell the SS supervisor all kinds of things to excuse my absence and promised them that I intended to work the following day. This man didn't show any anger; he seemed to be understanding, and he ordered the other two girls to help Mama carry the old shoes to me so that I could repair them

Mom returned to work with the girls after delivering my workload. After a couple of hours I expected Mama to bring my lunch ration -- a slice of bread (we called it `hay bread' that was not nourishing at all) usually with a spoonful of margarine and coffee. I was thirsty and feverish and could hardly wait for them. The door opened and Old Papa was standing there. He stooped because the door was shorter than he was. He had an aluminum dish in his hand and was looking for "die Kleine" (the little girl).

I was flabbergasted. He handed me the dish with hot tea and a slice of hard bread. I cried in my astonishment. This man wants to help me to get better!! A "Nazi" who had human feelings for a miserable dirty Jewess!!!

When Mama came with her ration and coffee I was reborn because in my tea was sugar, not saccharin. She couldn't believe her eyes. We shared the extra slice of bread and cried together for this miracle. The next day I reported to work as usual. I was now able to put on my shoes, but without the rags stuffed in them, because my feet were still swollen and numb.

Old Papa came as usual to check on us without any word of yesterday's absence or my sickness. There were other women there; he didn't want them to know of his generosity.

I could give many other examples of this unselfish man helping others without any ulterior motive. One of his greatest actions, which we found out about sooner than the others, concerned a woman who must have been pregnant before reaching Auschwitz. She was skinny; her dress was three sizes too big, and luckily she looked strong in Stutthof, so nobody knew that she was in her fourth month of pregnancy. She went out to work until the end of October when Old Papa noticed her changed figure.

He approached her one evening when she came back from work and told her to ask permission to stay home next day, because she was sick. The young woman was scared because she knew she would be killed if they found out that she was pregnant. She asked her bunkmates to help her to abort the child.

At the end of seven months of pregnancy, there was no way to hide this anymore. They decided that early in the morning, when everybody left for work, that they would go into the forest to cut trees and then have her lift the heaviest tree trunk after they brought it back. This would probably start the abortion. We shoemakers saw the group of women carrying a thick branch to her tent, but we had no idea how she could do it.

That morning Old Papa did not take attendance at the shoe factory because he had other things to do. He went alone to the forest and put together a wood cradle for the child he knew would be born in the camp. By the time he brought the cradle back to the young woman's tent the child was born, but within an hour it had died. He came to us with the bundle and told us to take it to the forest and bury it, and then he left. He looked very sad. Erika and I went to fulfill Old Papa's unusual order. When we were far enough from the camp, Erika dared to open the bundle. We were shocked at the sight, but we realized that we had to act fast.

The mother of the child told us the rest of the story when we visited her in the Revier tent for the sick. She said she had expected to be executed. She was looking hysterically for her child and she didn't know what the Nazis had done with him. She said she wanted to feed her baby.

Dr. Kardos yelled at her, "Shut up, you crazy irresponsible woman; you could bring about a big stink with your dead son. You will provoke the SS to kill us all as you did your son." And on and on.

Erika and I couldn't believe our ears. This doctor was a heartless Jewess who never had a child herself. We hated this woman. I approached her and confronted her with three words: "Just shut up. We'll take care of this suffering mother."

We then kneeled down on the floor where the mother was lying, exhausted, shaking and sweating, hallucinating feverishly, and still talking about her child. Erika told her that the baby would be all right; we had taken care of him. Now is the time for her to sleep -- relax so she can feed him when she is ready. I caressed her forehead, her trembling hand moving now slowly, then resting on the blankets. She fell asleep with a smile on her face, dreaming about her son.

We got up fast and left her to her dreams. We rushed to work, hoping nobody checked on us. There were more and more shoes and Mama and Elizabeth needed us. We lost at least one hour, but we thought we could hopefully save the mother.

Mama didn't have time to get coffee or lunch and Elizabeth was freezing. We sent her to bring us coffee and our lunch, and we worked non-stop until the field workers came back to the camp. Mama said Kaddish for the boy whom we buried. We visited the mother every day in the Revier and lied to her about her son. She didn't believe us, and by the third day was quite realistic and told us she wanted to hear the truth and that she'd cope with it. We had to tell her. She was still bleeding when the doctor sent her back to her tent; she needed the place for very sick people, not for women giving birth.

In Pearl S. Buck's novel *The Good Earth* the farmer's wife worked in the field and gave birth to her child, and an hour later continued to work carrying the newborn with her in a rag until the sun set.

The sick people needed some comforting words and kindness if they didn't get any medication, because there wasn't any for Jewish slaves. Dr. Kardos had a lot of guilt. Those who survived accused her of several crimes and prosecuted her for them after the war, even for crimes she did not commit. Unfortunately, the judges who were supposed to conduct a fair trial had no idea about the impossible lives we had led. They couldn't imagine what it was like in a Nazi concentration camp or in a slave labor camp in 1944 and 1945.

Those who prosecuted the doctor and those who defended her had the right to judge her, but the judges gave her three years prison in Jilava, an infamous underground prison in Romania. I went to her trial as a witness. There were others also who knew that she didn't have the means to really cure serious illnesses or the epidemic of paratyphoid, that she could only handle cuts, treat swelling with ice, prescribe rest in the Revier for a sprained ankle, wrist, or shoulder, or suggest coal for diarrhea. But she was rude, and frustrated by her helplessness.

After she returned from jail she found a job, but not as a doctor. In a communist society those who didn't work didn't eat, and she had to accept any kind of job. She applied to be a member of the Communist Party, but wasn't accepted. She died of depression and anorexia. She died like a pariah, and her husband also suffered with her until she passed away, isolated from everybody else.

The mother of the aborted child died in the Death March on January 20th, one day before the liberation.

Chapter Sixteen: Christmas, 1944

During the last week of November 1944, we buried close to seventy women in one grave close to the camp. The ground was so frozen, it had to be dynamited. How small the camps groups were becoming in the morning at roll call! Not even five hundred of the one thousand women were left, and only about four hundred could go out to the fields. Thirty or forty people, like us -- the shoe repairers, cooking staff, 'Revier' patients, the very sick, and those who could not even move — remained daily in the camp. There was less food, and smaller portions. Transporting food through the snow to the camp had become more difficult, and the war -- if it was possible -- had become more fierce. Now, we could hear cannons in the distance during the night, but we didn't know whose cannons they were. Our guards more anxiously pushed us to build obstacles against the rapidly approaching Red Army. Their anger found an outlet in yelling and beating us.

We did not believe we would survive December and January in this winter under these circumstances. The strong wind was rattling and shaking our tent. I could imagine how cold it was in the fields for those who worked there. The girls had to bundle themselves in two blankets held by strings ripped from their dresses. Their shoulders and arms were covered, but their hands had to be free to use their shovel or ax. They had to move constantly to keep blood circulating, but their cheeks were frostbitten Those who survived the camp -- those I've met at reunions in USA, Israel, and Romania -- are all victims of arthritis of the hands, feet, hips, and knees.

There were now days when no one was taken out for field-work because it was impossibly frigid. It was cold in the tents too, but at least it was not as windy as outside. I can still see the sight of hundreds of women in their bunks -- five up, five under -- sitting covered with their blankets, and if they had enough energy to sit up, killing lice with their fingernails. If not, they lay on the beds, listless, scratching, waiting for lunch when they had to get up and stay in line for hours for their one slice of bread. Then, for dinner, they had to stand on line again, because there was no way to distribute food to four hundred people inside the tents. You can see why I felt miserable and guilty that for the previous four weeks I had been privileged to stay in the camp and get food for the four of us, the shoe repairers, without having to stand on line.

They made us double our efforts to work on shoes. There were enough materials from old shoes to use for mending, and we asked for new sewing thread and needles every week when a supply truck would come with bread or potatoes. Wooden shoes could not be used in the snow, so the SS stopped ordering them. For Christmas they ordered fifty pairs, and we had to decide who needed the shoes most because theirs were beyond repair. It was difficult, if not impossible to make fair choices in such misery. All of us needed shoes, so we couldn't decide. Of course, we made everybody angry, and they blamed us for favoring our friends by giving them shoes..

The SS came and gave the last twenty pairs at random to whoever was luckiest. We were very frustrated because we knew who really needed shoes. I left the group, ran up to the cooking place, and hid behind a big cooking case, where I saw a potato. I kneeled down and tried to get it. Suddenly a Nazi not from our camp saw me and stood behind me. I froze in fear that he had caught me stealing. But he started to sing, "Es geht alles voruber." (Everything goes away, everything goes by, and after each December comes again a May). He put his finger on his lips, "Quiet, but you will see the song bears the truth." He let me take the potato and said, "Schnell! Arbeiten und essen." (Quick! Work and eat). I was amazed by his remarks but I felt that he knew the war would soon be over, and a new May would come.

Mama was surprised that the Nazi didn't beat me up. She was always concerned that I would get into trouble because I was always hungry and trying to get food by any means, so much so that sometimes I lost my common sense and took risks that could have cost me my life.

Although we prisoners were all Jews, we felt in the air that Christmas was coming. The Nazi guards probably hoped to be with their families, but not one got vacation leave for the holidays. Our Kapo, Aranka, told us that the cooks would prepare a special dinner for the Nazis and for us. We would even have some meat in our soup, but my mother said she didn't intend to eat any meat, no matter what kind because it was not kosher. By this time however she didn't tell me not to eat. We were really desperate to have something substantial in our stomach.

There was some excitement in the camp. The forest was beautiful as lots of pine trees had shining snow on them like decorations. Two guards cut a huge tree and asked five girls to pull it into their dining room. Yolan, my distant cousin, was among them. They were exhausted when they returned but they had great news for us. We met without my Mom because did not take part in our adventures. Instead, she gave her place to Leon, who was ready for everything and any risks.

Yolan described the inside of the dining room for Christmas Eve: "A long table for fifteen guards and Hitler youth, one of the wives and another 'girlfriend' were the two women. White tablecloths and real china, silverware, glasses, and paper napkins were on the long improvised tables. Yolan was so excited that her cheeks were burning. She thought of Friday night dinner with her family. Only the Challe was missing, she said, and the candle sticks with candles that her mother used to light and bless on Shabbat. We shared her excitement and listened intently. Then came the questioning for details.

Leon was the first: "What are the plans for the dinner? When will they decorate the tree? When will the actual eating take place? How many courses are on the menu? Is there any singing or dancing planned? Are there any musical instruments in the dining room?"

Erika interrupted and asked: "What do you care, Leon? You're not invited to sing Christmas carols."

Then I realized what was behind these questions. Leon looked at me. We were six girls who were ready. She asked, "Klara, are you coming?" I said yes.

Yolan knew from the beginning that we'd try to get out of the camp to the nearest village while this Christmas dinner was going on. How long would it last? How much time would it take to get to the nearest house? We didn't know. We would beg for food. The villagers might be generous on Christmas Eve. They must have known that we were hungry. And after all, we worked in their fields digging the trenches that would protect them from the Russians. We were sure that we would get something to eat. But when could we leave? When would the outside guard go to eat? Maybe when the guards changed they would go eat together and not worry about us. Where could we miserable prisoners go anyway?

We, the six, were sure that we would make it.

Mama found our group and told us that we should disperse because Aranka's sneaky sister, Susie (Zsuzsi) was watching us and was coming toward us. When she reached us she said to me: "Klari, you play the accordion, you will have to entertain the SS men with your playing at the dinner during the Christmas feast."

Did I have anything to say about it?

I wanted to tell her no, but instead I said, "Look, Zsuzsi, it is very flattering to amuse the Nazis, but I don't know how to play Christmas carols or German songs. I know one Richard Strauss waltz, but that will not satisfy their musical requirements for religious customs."

She did not believe me and called me a fool. I should be grateful, she said, because they might even give me a piece of bread or a piece of meat!

Leon kicked me and told me to go. She'd explain why later. "Of course," she said out loud, full of sarcasm in her voice, "Klara is happy to be invited to a party like this."

Again, Zsuzsi turned around and ran to her sister, her mission accomplished. Leon and I left them and I yelled at her, "Why do you push me into this mess?"

She pinched my arm and called me stupid. "But you could be our savior. You will go play," she ordered. "You will be kicked out if you don't know how to play, and you will tell us how much time we will possibly have for our escapade, and you will come with us too."

This inside information would be a great help. .

And so it happened. The real worry was on my Mama's fearful face. Oh God! How pale and sick she was. I could see her losing weight every day. The string around her waist was twice as long as a month ago as she pulled the coat closer and closer around her body. She said it "kept me warmer."

I felt like my heart would stop should something happen to her. How could I live without her? I was ready to tell the girls that I couldn't let mother suffer like this. She wouldn't survive if something happened to me.

When my mother saw this dilemma on my face, she said, "Go my child. Religion makes everybody do good. They will give you food, and you need it. Just be careful and don't be greedy. I'll wait for you. I won't worry."

Our hunger made us forget our pride. So we will be beggars, but maybe we'll have something in our stomachs. What's that word -- dignity? There was no such thing in our vocabulary anymore.

I had two deep pockets in my coat dress that I had worn since November, when the previous owner died. It was just two thin cloths to wear out in the trenches. The pockets served many purposes, but mainly to hide food. Lately, I had to bring my bread ration into my workplace because everybody was out to steal. They were all hungry: sisters stole from each other; mothers and daughters argued for the bigger slice of bread, others even counted the number of spoonfuls of soup or coffee who drank more gulps and who less. But there had never been such a dispute between me and my Mom. I was planning already in the camp how much food I could bring to her in my big pockets. My blanket would cover everything.

Christmas dinner for us was no different from any other night, except some pieces of meat here and there in the soup and it was thicker. The next day we found out that the meat was horsemeat, and it wasn't even good horsemeat. We also received a two inch thick piece of bread, and marmalade, which was sweet. We saved it for the next day because we hoped to eat cake or Brioche, which was a European custom to have on this eve.

We were so excited with our plans that we didn't even notice that our Kapo, Aranka, had come to us, her face shining. She had so much margarine that she had put some on her face also. She had a white scarf starched like a nurse's. She had used flour to starch it. Where she had gotten it I did not know. And she smelled of soup. I didn't know how she could have got that either. Her long dress was incredibly clean, like it came from the cleaners.

She was not too happy to have to take me with her to the SS party, but she would get good points for herself by having some kid entertain the guards of the universe, our SS men. She looked at me critically but could find no fault in my appearance. She asked if I had a lot of lice, or if I had killed them all for the occasion. I told her I hadn't counted them today, but definitely had more than she did, because she had more time to deal with them.

Leon saw me leaving and signaled to me, "Come back as soon as you can."

It was dark already, but I waved to her. "I will".

I entered the well-lit room. There were loud voices and lots of food on the tables. I smelled the roasted pork that my Christian friends used to prepare at their houses for Christmas. We waited for a while in the corner until an SS got up and gave Aranka his accordion to hand to me. It was bigger than mine at home, and much heavier – a one hundred twenty button bass to be supported by just my left hand. I had never played on such a monster.

It pulled down my skinny shoulders, and my frozen fingers hardly moved on the keys of my right hand. I tried first without sound, just moving my fingers to warm up. Then I waited for a signal. I seemed to be the only musician, but didn't know if the SS guard had played already or not.

I was terribly excited and afraid. On the one hand, I wanted to be kicked out as soon as possible. On the other, I would be ashamed if I made a fool of myself, or was seen as a show-off who said she played the accordion but knew nothing. I didn't give a damn about their laughter or sarcasm, but I cared for my integrity as a Jewess who doesn't lie, unlike the Nazis.

They all started to drink and eat hot knockwurst with bread and sauerkraut, and the saliva started to flow in and out of my mouth, but I controlled my empty stomach's growls. I was thinking of the goodies that we would eat after we begged from the farmers.

I tried to study this accordion. How will I play this huge instrument? Then I panicked. Aranka watched my movements, as if it would be her fault I couldn't play.

"Pull yourself together," she said, "and start to play. You see them looking at you."

So I tuned in Strauss's *An der schönen blauen Donau op. 314* commonly known as the *Blue Danube* waltz. There were parts I played well, but my left hand was constantly searching for the buttons to get the right keys. Just the waltz as written was not enough for me. I heard the false B-flat that I kept touching. But I always did well under pressure, so I overcame my fear. Then my fingers warmed up and my thoughts went back to my sixteenth birthday party and my father dancing with my mother while they watched me with pride. (My father only danced the waltz and the csardas, the Hungarian national dance, and the Romanian hora.) I loved to dance with my father. He sang along with the music. He was strong, and it was easy to follow his steps and he had a perfect sense of rhythm. But here nobody got up to dance, though they listened, and their feet tapped the tempo.

I grew calmer and played on, repeating sections of the *Blue Danube*. When I finished, I looked at Old Papa, our SS friend. I saw him smiling and clapping his hands. Some others followed, clapping condescendingly, and they asked me to play the German national anthem, *Das Lied der Deutschen* (the Song of the Germans) also known by its first line as *Deutschland Uber Alles*.

I lowered my head, and said that in Hungary I was not taught that, and could not play it. They said I could play other Christmas carols instead, even though the Jews crucified Jesus. So I played "O Tannenbaum," but they wanted religious carols and I didn't know any.

The owner of the accordion came to me and said with sarcasm, "Well, I know you cannot learn them tonight. You can leave and relax. Next year, if you live, you'll play only German songs."

Aranka had got into a conversation with one of the women and didn't notice that I had left the dining room. Nobody gave me any food, but when I rushed out through the kitchen, the cook, who was a Jewess, gave me a bone on which there was some meat.

It was pitch dark. The snow was hard and cracked under my steps, making a lot of noise. I didn't see any guards, but behind the first tent I saw the shadows of the five girls walking towards me. My friends asked me about the possibilities of getting out of the camp, and I said, "Now or never."

The SS hadn't started dinner yet. I had seen no guards around, and the moon was just a crescent. I didn't know the time, but figured we would have an hour and a half to get back before the end of their dinner. If we were lucky, the farmhouses would not be very far from the camp, one or two miles at most.

I wanted to take my blanket from the tent and hug my mother goodbye, but Leon jumped at me, saying, "Here is your blanket; and your mother knows we would leave just as soon as you came from the SS."

I believed it, and reluctantly agreed to follow Leon's leadership. We went to the edge of the forest one by one, like geese, trying to find the route to the village. There was no obstacle whatsoever, and we stepped out fast in the opposite direction, not where we usually marched to the fields to dig the anti-tank trenches. After about five hundred yards, we reached an unpaved road where the snow was only two to three inches deep. We could tell carriages or even trucks usually used this road, because we felt the big tire marks. We were hopeful that we would find the village.

Maybe after a mile, we saw lights coming from little houses. We didn't stop at the first house but we went on until we saw a quiet street and we could not hear singing, or any noise. There we decided to split into groups of two and knock on different house doors to avoid depleting any one house. We saw at least ten to fifteen houses in this tiny street. Leon and I stuck together; the other four girls made two groups. We agreed to meet in the forest as soon as possible if we got some food.

The first house on our right was open. An old lady came to the door. She said she heard us talking, but could not tell which language we were speaking. She thought we were escaped prisoners -- those who dug trenches to avoid the Russian tanks. She felt sorry for us. The guards had kept this little community away from us. The old lady gave us bread, some brioche, two small hamburgers, and some boiled potatoes she had just peeled.

There were no men in her house, only her daughter and three grandchildren. She didn't want us to come in because the children would be afraid of our looks with the blankets and strings around our necks. We understood, thanked her for her generosity, and then left.

Leon continued to the next house, maybe twenty yards from the first. We had become real beggars by now. The families never looked at us. There was always a woman who came to the door and quickly gave us food, then pushed us out as fast as she could so we could not bother her family and upset their holiday.

In two houses, there was food prepared in the window for the carol singers who were expected to come later. There were nut cakes rolled into twelve inch lengths, two inches thick, and it would be very easy to carry them in our pockets. As the woman of the house brought us bread, potatoes and chicken legs, Leon and I took a couple of the best cakes. Leon looked at the knife that was with the cakes. We had not had one since Auschwitz.

Leon asked the knife, "Will you come with me?" but the knife did not answer. "Then, I will take you anyway," she said, and used it to cut a handsome portion of the cake which she put in her pocket.

I almost burst out laughing as she spoke to the knife and mimicked the question, but we had to go. Time was running out and we had to get back to the camp. If I recall correctly, we had gone to four or five houses and were refused only by one grouchy old man who closed the door in our faces, saying that he knew who we were: hungry, dirty Jews who deserved their misfortune.

We felt our pockets full and our stomachs, too. Now I could bring all my treasure to my Mama. I was satisfied and ready to return. Leon agreed. We were frozen anyway, so we marched quickly towards the edge of the forest where the other two girls were waiting to meet us. They had not seen Yolan or Elizabeth. We waited for them for awhile but we were afraid we would get in trouble getting back to the camp so late.

We started off slowly, constantly looking back, until we saw the shadows of the two girls running toward us in the faint moonlight. We could see the dim light of the camp and we tiptoed to our tent. The others found their places, too. Elizabeth came five minutes later, crying in the dark.

She whispered, "The guard caught Yolan, and he shot in the air when he realized that she was a prisoner and not a Russian spy." Elizabeth did not know what had happened since then, and we had no idea what to do next.

Mama woke up and looked at us. All this happened so quickly that no one asked if the inmates were aware of our arrival. One woman, Manci, who had been sick for a long time with a high fever, used to talk in her sleep. She was screaming now all the time about her husband and lovemaking. She yelled about how hungry she was, and how she wanted a man. Engel, the SS-man, was in her dream coming to her bed, and she yelled, "Kom zu mir, Engel. Du hast so schone mund. ("Come to me, Engel. You have such a beautiful mouth and lips.") This is what we heard all the time. Mama told me that this won't last long: poor Munci will soon die if the SS didn't carry her away to the tent where all the other terminally ill are already.

Meanwhile, we couldn't sleep without knowing what had happened to Yolan. I opened the tent door; it was a paper thin wooden door that made funny noises when the hinges moved. I stared out in the dark. In the middle of the hill where we used to get our dinner close to the kitchen, I saw Yolan tied to the column that supported the roof over the four big cans in which our meals were cooked.

Not far from Yolan, a guard was pacing right and left, pouring water on his only prisoner -- on Christmas night! What was he doing, torturing her? We found out later that she had been lying on the snow. The guard found her and tied her to the column and started pouring cold water from a bucket onto her to wake her up. The noise woke up the prisoners from the first tent.

I tried to run out to her from my tent. I ran with three other girls to Yolan; we were all flabbergasted by how the guard was tormenting Yolan because she was caught with food in her pocket -- the beggar that went out to the village, "ruining the reputation" of the SS camps. The guard was yelling and cursing all this time, until he saw us. We begged him to let us carry Yolan into the tent while she was still alive. Her body was frozen with cold water that was dripping from her blanket, but she was still breathing. The guard chased us away, shouting that the whole camp should see her in the morning to learn a lesson.

I took a risk and challenged him, saying that morning was still far away. He said it was already four o'clock and they would soon be changing guards; the next guard would also deal with this swine. We all begged him to have mercy on this girl; we might be able to save her. After all, it's Christmas morning.

He turned his back to us, and so we picked up Yolan. She was terribly heavy with all the ice on her. We carried her to the nearest tent and I pulled off her clothing and started to gently rub her fingers with cold water to revive her, and the others started to move her lips and legs. Mama helped us.

Yolan's eyelids started to open, and she warmed up. She opened her eyes and looked at us, surprised and incredulous.

Elizabeth talked to her quietly. "When the guards caught you I was ten steps ahead of you. When I looked back, you were nowhere."

Yolan responded, "When you stepped into the tent, the guard heard the noise, and I was there."

But we could hardly hear this sentence. She couldn't really talk or move. She remained rigid for hours. Finally she raised her hand, but her legs were still stiff like wooden sticks. How would she survive? We didn't know it then but we only had twenty-five days until we would march from the camp, chased by our guards, in a death march. It remains another puzzle, very much like a miracle. Today she is crippled, married to a Christian, immigrated to Israel, and has two successful, healthy children.

Chapter Seventeen:
Last Days in Guttau

Christmas day of 1944 ended with Yolan's frozen body exposed in the most visible point of our camp. Four girls and I pulled her to the closest tent and worked on reviving her. The prisoners found out that we had gone out to the village and had begged for food, and they blamed us, saying that we deserved whatever punishment we got. Luckily, the SS guards were busy with more serious problems -- the Russians were approaching victoriously to our region -- so they forgot about us and were getting ready to evacuate our camp, which was not easy, as they did not want to leave any trace of their horrible, inhuman treatment of their enslaved prisoners.

We only heard rumors of our leaving the camp to go to another place to continue the digging. This seemed impossible! There were now only two hundred women who could walk, out of the one thousand who left Stutthof in

August 1944. There remained between seventy and eighty dying people in one tent while another tent was full of dead bodies that we could not bury because of the frozen ground. From the first of January, there had hardly been a day when we could go out into the fields.

We shoe repairers worked twelve hours a day to prepare the shoes for the needy in an eventual evacuation. Four more girls helped us cut up old shoes and use the parts to mend the ones that would be used. Out of these two hundred women, fifty did not have shoes or only had wooden shoes. It was a terrible situation. The snow was falling and the frost was unbearable. Our wood supply from the forest was decreasing. We had to go farther into the forest to cut branches to heat our tents.

We found a newspaper around the kitchen dated December 21st that said the Russians had crossed the border of East Prussia and were advancing quickly in spite of the winter conditions. The article said that the German army would stop the Russians; there was no question about that. We hoped that this was all propaganda and that the Germans would lose the war. But who would survive?

The last couple of weeks in every bunk there was someone who died unnoticed, and in the morning women would wake to find a cold body beside them.

Mama used to wake me up saying, "Are you all right? Are you all right?"

I would say, "Why do you ask?" And she would reply that she could not hear me breathing. "You never snore!"

"Yes," I would reply, "but I breathe!"

Then I would go back to sleep, and she would come close to my back to feel my breathing on her chest. She did not sleep. She was watching me.

The lethal paratyphoid fever was spreading so fast that no one was safe from the danger. Very few could eat -- only drink. The minute they ate something, it went right through their system. Then high fever weakened their resistance and they died.

On January 7th (I know the date because it was the old SS man's birthday) Old Papa came to us shoe repairers and inspected the number of usable shoes we had made that day, because it was urgent that we leave the camp and find a better place to dig anti-tank ditches. He told us that he would not celebrate his birthday now because he hoped that pretty soon he would be with his family with whom he could enjoy a party. He promised us bigger pieces of sole and more thread to work with. We would have to make more usable shoes.

He said, "No human being can walk in this weather barefooted."

I asked, "Are we human beings?"

He looked at me with sheepish eyes and said, "You will be some time."

He kept his promise, and the next day he brought big bags of mending materials and we worked feverishly, producing as much as we could as fast as we could.

Mama's fingers were frozen and we all saved our hot coffee to warm our fingers in our wooden dishes. We comforted ourselves saying that we were not missing anything because the coffee tasted so terrible.

Three days later, the SS men brought dynamite to create one big hole in which to bury about thirty corpses. This meant thirty blankets for those who were still dragged off to dig trenches. What a tragic day. My group only wept inside our tent working on shoes while the others were pushed to finish the burial and cover the grave so that the bodies on top could not be seen. The rest of the corpses would be buried in two weeks, but there was no time for that now.

We were evacuated on the 19th of January. We could not finish all the shoes that were needed because on the 18th (the day before my birthday) in the afternoon, we heard a voice on the loudspeaker telling us to gather immediately in the "appel" (roll call) where we would have early dinner distribution on account of the bad weather.

That day no one went out to work. Instead, everybody stayed in the cold tents. Some still had wood to burn but no one was allowed to go and cut more in the forest. The girls washed themselves with snow and killed the lice in their clothing. Others covered themselves in blankets. Some had two or three blankets depending on how many friends of theirs had died, and they slept all day. Nobody saw our "leaders," the Kapo, her sisters, or their aides. They knew something, but did not tell us to avoid creating panic. What could we do? Rebel? Strike? Protest? This was ridiculous even to imagine. In the Revier the very sick were left to their suffering. They did not even have water or heat. Dr. Kardos was away meeting with the SS and the Jewish leaders. Our early dinner was distributed on a very dark afternoon. It looked as if it would snow again.

Aranka looked very pale as she gave orders to proceed with the distribution of our soup, which was unusually thick, full of potato peels, carrots, and other vegetables like turnips. Turnips were cattle food, but we were very happy to be given some. It seemed to be the Last Supper without Leonardo DaVinci painting us. Then they gave us a big ration of bread, one and one-half inches thick, and said we could eat it because we would get another portion tomorrow.

The order came from the SS leader that the next day we should put on all our clothing and the blankets and carry our dishes and spoons with us after breakfast, because we would leave early in the morning. Where? Nobody knew. We would get orders in the morning.

Austräten! We dispersed with our precious dinners. This meal was more important than whatever might occur the next day which I had forgotten was my eighteenth birthday. That evening, Mama and I, the two Blau sisters and Leon prepared all our belongings for tomorrow in just five minutes.

Aranka and her sister, Susie, needed the whole night to pack all what of they had. Unfortunately, the thirty big breads (ten portions for ten people) that were hidden under straw in their tent had begun to rot and could not be taken. They had saved provisions by stealing from us every day and giving us smaller and smaller portions at distribution. Another thing they were hiding was margarine wrapped in paper. It was so frozen that they could easily carry a pound, but they were afraid to eat it in front of us. They were right, of course, our hungry crowd would have killed them.

We saw this at night in very dim light. We had enough wood to last till morning. After all, we were privileged because we happened to share Aranka's tent. Realizing that even our Jewish leader cheated and stole from us was a terrible blow. Our food! Leon could hardly hold her temper. If it were not the day before the new unknown, she said, she would have ordered a group to join her in beating them up. But now, she could only spit on them and call them thieves of human lives.

January 19th came with a roll call earlier than five o'clock. Mama was very weak and very excited and her cheeks were burning. She was half the size she had been nine months before. She knew it was my birthday, and she could not wait any longer with her surprise. When everybody was busy counting us, she pulled out a package wrapped in newspaper from under her two layers of blankets.

"Happy Birthday, my darling," she said. "I want you to know how happy you have made my life all these years, and how grateful I am to my God for your existence." She hugged me and we both cried. The three people in our line were curious about what was in the newspaper. I opened it, and Mama said, "It's a birthday cake." It was three portions of bread put together in layers with margarine in between. It was four inches high and stuck together -- the greatest present in my life. I cried like a baby, although I wondered where she had got all the bread.

"Mama," I looked at her and asked, "Where did you find this treasure?" She was evasive, and said that I, her daughter, did not eat my ration one day because we had been given a good soup.

"Mama," I said, "you are not telling the truth. I am so hungry all the time that I could eat a stone!"

She had not eaten her portion of bread for three days in order to make this layer cake for my birthday. She smiled and hugged me again, but did not lie anymore. She was a mother in all circumstances, the best one could ever have. The girls cried with us and I felt sorry for them. They did not know when or if they would have their mother's love again. In fact, they never saw their mothers after Auschwitz.

We did not eat the cake because there was no time. We were ordered to get ready, turn left, and begin marching on the road that we had used to go to the trenches. We could hear the loud roar of the canons behind us. Now we knew that the Russians were coming and we had to evacuate before they reached us. They must have been only twenty or thirty kilometers away.

What we did not understand then was why Dr. Kardos, two nurses, and three or four SS men remained in the camp only to follow us a half hour later with a carriage in which the SS luggage was carried. They had stayed behind to inject the very sick, as many of them as they could, with poison. The SS killed the rest with their weapons. Even so, ten or twelve survived until the Russians came and brought them to hospitals and cured them in the Soviet Union. We knew this because they came home to us eight months later and told us of their terrible ordeal.

Chapter Eighteen:
Death March

After the first five hundred yards we realized that walking in this weather on the frozen snow and ice required superhuman abort. Gray skies predicting more snow were somewhat more comforting. Maybe it would become less cold. We were not marching in lines of five anymore, and had almost lost contact with the other girls in our row. We were a herd of animals without a herdsman. The SS did not give a damn if someone fell and could not get up.

"Los, weiter!" (Fast, go on!)

They yelled when a friend would try to help someone up, and the guards would raise their guns, but did not shoot. They did not want to waste their ammunition, so they let these miserable creatures fall and stay behind.

"They will follow us if they want to," they said. "They are just lazy trouble makers."

After two miles I looked back and did not see some of the people who had been close to me including Babuci, her mother, and two sisters who used to work in the trenches with my group, Oli, my classmate from the Jewish school, my math teacher from the ninth grade, and others. Dr. Kardos and her crew from the Revier caught up with us after an hour or so.

We dragged ourselves like mules carrying their bodies as luggage, moving as slowly as the lice in our clothing. Unfortunately, my mother's left shoe fell apart. She did not have time to repair it before our departure. I ripped a piece from the length of my blanket, and, like a belt, wrapped it around her shoe three or four times to protect her feet from the snow. She was limping now because her left shoe was higher than the right one. She hung on, though, and did not complain -- just prayed silently. She kept saying, "You will have better birthdays than this, my dear child."

When Mama felt like stopping, if only for a minute, I would not let her. When I said I could not move anymore, she pushed me to go on. "We will freeze if we fall in the snow," she said.

We looked like scarecrows with our dark gray blankets covering our heads and our noses and with the string around our necks holding the blankets together. The SS urged us to go faster by cracking their whips, but they did so in vain. Their snapping sounded to us like sirens of the last call. We could march no more.

We stopped in an empty, open barn without a roof, and collapsed, but we only rested about an hour there, and had to continue until late that night. We reached another barn, this one with a roof above us and some straw under our feet. We were frozen, hungry, and exhausted. We ate the last crumbs of the "birthday cake" with some drops of coffee mixed with snow at the bottom of our dishes. Then we sat on the straw, leaned on each other's shoulders, and tried to sleep.

The SS woke us up. "Schnell (Quick)! Get up, we have to find a place to sleep."

The whips cracked again, and we moved. I could not see anybody in the dark, but I am sure a few people remained. Babuci and her mother were not with us any more. Ten months after liberation we found out they had collapsed in the middle of the road. A Polish carriage had picked them up, but an SS horseman pulled them from the carriage and wanted to shoot them. Babuci's mother spoke perfect German and begged him to spare their lives. In the middle of this, the Polish man took off with his carriage. When the SS man realized this, he took off after the carriage, but the Pole escaped.

Babuci and her mother waited until dark and walked to a house where they saw smoke. They were liberated there by Russians, whose leader was a Jewish captain. He ordered the Polish couple to feed them, delouse, and clean them. Eventually they were taken to Russia and came home at the end of August 1945, after having been treated in a hospital.

On the second day of the march, our group of about one hundred fifty continued during the night until we reached another barn with a roof. There was some straw there, horse food, dry grass and nothing else. We all got in and sat close to one another. We fell asleep in that position without eating or drinking anything. The SS woke us up early in the morning and pushed us into lines. Behind the barn, one hundred fifty women emptied their bladders and their infected intestines.

We marched that whole day hungry, thirsty, and dehydrated. Many of us were freezing to death. We did not look back anymore, just dragged ourselves along the icy road. There were very few vehicles on that road. The SS had ordered the Polish peasants to keep away from us, and relentlessly pushed us along. They realized, as did we, that if we stopped, we would not be able to get up again.

It was pitch dark when we noticed some tiny lights in the distance. With our last bit of strength, we started walking faster. Mama pulled on my blanket and I held onto her. The lights came closer. In a half a mile, we saw a farm house with a bigger stable and heard the sounds of animals. Our minds were numb. Nobody talked; nobody cried.

When we reached the farm, Aranka pulled ten women who could still move from the group and pushed us into the house to cook the SS some food. The rest went with one petroleum lamp to the huge stable to determine where they would sleep.

The kitchen was big, but the guards occupied all the benches and chairs, and they ordered us to begin cooking soup. We could barely stand on our feet. We found a tiny pantry containing enough food for a small family who had either run away, or was still hiding somewhere in the house. The cook from our camp found some potatoes, lard, and carrots in the pantry, and ordered us to peel them. Mama and I were so exhausted we could only cry when a knife was handed to us.

Someone found some chicory and in no time there was coffee on the table for the SS guards. Old Papa took a pitcher and came to the room where we were, and gave us a drink. I'll never forget the taste of that coffee. It was out of this world. We started to warm up and looked for a corner where we could get some sleep. There was no sound from the stable and no light. Some canned foods were opened in the kitchen; soon we heard the guards praising the liver pâté.

Later, we woke up in the middle of the night and heard a big discussion in the kitchen. Aranka was sitting in the middle of the pantry and whispered, "Shut up," in Hungarian.

We heard one SS asking what should be done with this herd of sick people. After a while an answer came from another. "Let's burn them. There is enough straw in the stable."

Two others shouted, "You're crazy! The whole region will smell of burning flesh."

Another suggestion came, "Let's shoot them."

Now we heard Old Papa's voice, "That's the worst idea, to waste our ammunition on them. How will we protect ourselves when the Russians arrive?" And he added, "The hell with them. I would leave them here in the middle of nowhere, and we should leave this place as soon as possible."

There was dead silence after this. We tried to listen, but we fell asleep again, exhausted and hungry. I don't remember my dream, but Mama whispered in my ear and put her hand on my mouth, "Klarika," she said, "please keep calm or you'll wake everyone up, and the SS will throw us out into the courtyard.

I could hardly understand her words; I only felt the panic in her voice. I must have had a nightmare and was shivering with fever.

Very soon after, there was some commotion in the SS rooms, and then dead silence again. We did not know what time it was, but it was still dark, so we fell asleep again. When we woke up the sun was shining into the kitchen. The cook, Ester, rushed to search for coffee to give the SS, but their room was empty. There was no trace of them.

We were alive -- without guards!

We ran from the house to the stable and woke everyone saying, "Get up! We are free! The SS left us! No guards!"

Everybody was shouting, yelling, and jumping out from the straw into the courtyard. We could not believe our eyes. We were free! It was January 21, 1945, somewhere in the middle of nowhere, and we were on an empty farm abandoned by the Germans as they ran away from the Russian soldiers.

Rachel and Robert, your Dad was born exactly ten years later on January 21, 1955, the happiest day of my life.

Chapter Nineteen: Free of SS Guards - The Beginning of Our Journey Home

Not a soul was around, only some restless animals. A cow was mooing, but who knew how to milk one? Small pigs, but how do you eat them? There weren't any small animals like chickens or hens, and we hadn't seen any other barn or house in the horizon.

Some of the girls who came to the kitchen, took the knives, pots, and pans, found matches to make a fire with the branches and straw from the barn. Mama found some rice in the pantry and cooked it on the stove in spite of Aranka's yelling at her, but it was only enough for two or three people. Somehow, though, Mama made ten portions out of it by adding sunflower oil. Those who had severe diarrhea got a portion of it while the other girls killed small pigs.

We could hardly wait until the pork cooked on the outside fire, and we ate the meat without bread or vegetables. Of course, Mama wouldn't touch it because it wasn't kosher. Most of the girls became sick from the pork because they ate it on an empty stomach. Then we went on a search for food in the house, in the cellar, the pantry -- everywhere. Some carrots and turnips were left in the ground around the house, and we dug those out.

The sun was shining and the skies were blue. We heard the noise of a motorbike, and very soon a soldier appeared. We all ran towards him. He stopped and looked very surprised, then smiled and said something we didn't understand, but the Czech girls did. They jumped on him, and kissed and hugged this unshaven, dirty, tired, young Russian soldier.

He kept saying something like, "Others are coming too. We will win this war soon, and everybody will be free of Nazis. But watch out -- they are hiding everywhere and cause a lot of damage."

He didn't know who we were or why we were so sickly and skinny! We were the first Jewish group he had met, and we looked like skeletons.

We hoped the Russians would not arrive too late to liberate us. When Aranka told the soldier that we were the few survivors of a thousand women who were alive in August, and our group only numbered one hundred fifty, he became saddened. He couldn't help us in anything; he was the front of his group, but many others would follow in trucks, motorbikes, and on foot, he said.

He left us then, and nobody else came the whole afternoon. We were waiting for them but our hopes faded during every hour that passed. What should we do with this new freedom in the middle of nowhere? We found a bag of barley in the cellar, but we wouldn't eat it for hours, and mainly gave it to the sick who had eaten the pork and had suffered terribly from stomach pains. We also found corn ears. We couldn't wait until it was fully cooked, so we ate it while it was still hard. We went to sleep exhausted from our search of food, aching from eight months of suffering.

The next day more soldiers came, but they couldn't help us either. They were hungry, too. Some of them had been in the war for four years. They gave us some raw salted beef. One soldier, when he saw Mama's shoes, gave her a pair of soccer shoes two sizes bigger than her feet. I can't express how happy I was, no matter how ridiculous they looked, although with the cleats on the bottom, I didn't know how hard it would be for her to walk with them.

Mama's ankles were swollen. We hoped to get her some better shoes somewhere on our trip home.

One soldier showed us a map, pointing out the area where we were and where Transylvania was. It was Hungary when we were deported; now it was Romania. What was going on there right now on January 22, 1945, we did not yet know. It was still war, we heard.

"But the Germans are the losers. Pretty soon they will be kaput," the young soldier said.

We asked for his map, but he couldn't give it to us, because it was the only one he had. He showed us a road that would lead to a village, but he did not know how many hours it would take to walk there. Mentally, we were ready for any walk towards home, but physically, it was impossible. And the more we rested, the weaker we felt; we slept long hours, now, even during the daytime. We realized that our situation needed to be changed because here was no more food, no washing facilities, and everybody was getting sick. We needed medicine, doctors, and care.

I felt weak too, and somewhat feverish, and I thought that this was a reaction to my excitement of the last few days with the arrival of our long-dreamt-of freedom and the unknown future.

Three days later our group of fifteen made a decision to leave the place and explore new territory. The weather was still wintery, but not as cold as it had been the previous three or four days. We told everybody about our plan. Many said that they would like to go with us, but were not yet ready. They had to rest even if they had nothing to eat, they said; they were so weak and lacked energy. They could not face their family in this condition when they met them, they said.

This shows how ignorant we were about the events and conditions of our people since June 1st when we were at Auschwitz. We hoped that we would get home to our families, of course, but we couldn't believe that our grandparents could have survived these atrocities and forced labor. Mama and I strongly believed that my father would wait for us. All her brothers were young -- between forty and fifty -- and hard working men. My father's family, also younger than my father, could put up with hardship, too, we believed, and all of us would be reunited. As you see, we were beginning to think about our future, but our present was still very unpredictable.

The next day, we got up early in the morning, boiled some water with chicory coffee, ate some barley that we had cooked the night before, and took with us two big turnips for the road. We put on all the clothing we had. We put straw in our shoes to keep our feet warm.

We said goodbye to everybody, crying and hugging each other, and promised that somehow, somewhere we would meet again. By the time we left the farm, the sun was shining and the snow was reflecting its rays like tiny diamonds. We walked easily on the road -- talking, laughing, and singing, with no SS around, free and hopeful that something good would happen to us. For a while we were all alone on the road. Nothing broke the silence.

Then a truck came and did not stop. Russian soldiers in uniforms were in a hurry. Other trucks came, and finally, one stopped. A man started to ask questions. Two girls spoke some Russian; they found out from the soldier that we were approaching a village that was three or four hours away. We should try to get to a school that had a dormitory where we could sleep, he said. He was transporting ammunition, but he said there would be some trucks that might have room to take a couple of girls in the direction we were going. He gave us five loaves of Russian bread to divide among us. It wasn't fresh, but it was heavy, good, brown bread. We enjoyed every crumb of it.

One loaf for five girls! It filled us up and we continued our march with renewed energy.

I don't have a journal of the daily events of our three-month struggle to reach our home, but I will try to describe the most incredible experiences that stand out in my mind. Late one afternoon, we saw a couple of dim street-lights from a small village. The streets were empty; only two or three stores were open, with very few people. When we stopped in front of a store, we attracted curious eyes, as if we were from another planet.

We only asked one question: "Where is the school?"

They pointed in the direction, but they would not talk to us. They were Polish, and we had asked them in German. They despised the Germans, so they refused to speak their language. When we reached the school, it was dark. We found the dormitory with about fifteen bunk beds in it. All had straw mattresses covered with cotton sheets. We were just ready to settle down when Russian soldiers appeared at the door. We felt secure—they had liberated us. But they were too friendly; they hugged and kissed us, and after a while we guessed their true intentions. We pushed them away and screamed, until their officer appeared. He was a captain. He spoke quickly, and our two girls who spoke Russian could hardly understand him. He looked at Mama, the oldest and the slimmest woman, and asked her if she spoke Yiddish. Mama's pale face lit up. She said, "Of course. We are Jews, liberated by you from the Nazi concentration camps." The captain who had saved us told us he was Jewish too.

After this, our lives completely changed. For eight or nine days we were looked after and helped in whatever way the captain could. He chose me to go with a soldier to peasants' houses to ask for food, spices, dishes, towels, soap, and whatever clothing they could spare, and bring it to school. I wanted to take along the Czech girl to communicate better, but she was so weak and sickly she said she would rather rest.

The next day the soldier and I went to the village with a bed sheet as a bag and collected everything that the villagers were willing to give to beggars. They were poor, hard working people who were fed up with the Nazi occupation, the war, and their losses. Most of them were ignorant of what was going on in the world. They didn't read the newspapers or listen to the radio.

They looked at me with curiosity and when I tried to explain to them by gesturing and showing them my clothes and counting on my fingers how many girls were in the school, they gave me what they could spare. There were two or three houses where the people shut their doors in our faces, but then the soldier's authority came in handy. He banged on the door with his gun, which he carried on his shoulder, and the doors suddenly opened.

Those houses often belonged to the people who could afford to give much more, but were arrogant and full of hatred. By the end of the day, we had food for everybody -- we could even cook a potato soup for the soldiers with very big potatoes. We all ate the evening dinner after washing our hands with soap and warm water. Unfortunately, some of the soldiers got drunk at night on vodka and broke into our dormitory. We escaped rape again with the help of our Jewish captain, who placed a guard in front of our door and punished the intruders. From then on, we no longer had trouble with them.

One night, the captain asked us to join him in the school's "auditorium" where we saw a piano. The captain played and sang Yiddish songs and we sang along. He also played Beethoven's *Ode to Joy*. Together, we all wished the war would be over and peace would prevail.

We knew we had to leave soon, but I will never forget those first days of our freedom in an empty school. Where were the students and teachers? We didn't know. Lots of books, mainly German, were in the middle of some classrooms. Some were unpacked and left behind by the administrators who did not care, but just ran away from the Russians.

From then on, we had backpacks that we carried with us filled with one or two panties, a pair of socks, a towel, some baked potatoes, a knife, a metal spoon, and a glass or cup full of water or soup. We still had our clothing and blankets for coats, with our lice in them. They hadn't disappeared despite our clothes washing. Mama still hadn't any better shoes, so she walked in her soccer cleats. Her ankles were swollen again after two hours of marching, yet she kept going.

It was already February, and we still had not seen any liberated prisoners from other camps. Our group was smaller now. Three or four girls chose to go to the east, while others remained in the village. About fourteen of us chose to go southwest to find a town which could give us more shelter or transportation "home."

It took us three hours to reach the outskirts of Neumark, a small town filled with smoke and fires. In the middle of the day in the marketplaces, we saw beautiful tree-lined streets in front of pretty brick houses with flowers in the windows. But there were piles of books burning in the streets, and there were huge piles of wooden house columns smoking everywhere. This was the disaster caused by the Germans who burned everything rather than leave anything behind for the Russians. They had run away -- who knew where. Store doors were opened. People were looting everything that they could put their hands on and were running around seemingly with no direction.

We had a hard time passing through these streets. I couldn't look away from the beautiful burning books: Heine, Goethe, Thomas Mann. I can still remember the golden titles on the books in the flames. What a crime to burn these books, I thought. We ran as fast as we could to get out of this burning, smoky town. I hoped we would soon find another village or farm and forget the destruction. After fifty years, I can still see the burning town as vividly than ever.

We saw people running in various directions and we followed those who ran to a major intersection which led to a road packed with horse-drawn carriages, some were covered by tents, some were open with children bundled up in winter clothes.

How we envied them!

They looked at us with curious eyes. They didn't know who these sickly looking girls were with uniforms on, numbers on their clothes, running for their lives. They didn't take the time to find out who we were, they didn't care. But one girl, around my age, yelled from the carriage in German, "Go to the right; there are still Nazis there. To the left there are Russians." Obviously she did not know we were running away from the Nazis. But this was a help, although unintended, we were grateful to her. To her surprise, we turned immediately to the left.

We slowed down, but walked steadily until we could no longer see people or carriages around us. We stopped on the side of the road in a snow covered ditch; the sun was still shining and we were free to do whatever we felt like doing. We were tired, hungry, filled with experiences that we had to sort out in our rusty minds.

After an hour or so we realized we had to locate a place to sleep -- and before sunset. We pulled ourselves together and returned to the road.

Our days and nights were very similar for many days in February. We walked during the day and slept in attics, stables, or empty farmhouses at night. If we were lucky, some villagers were kind and gave us some thick warm soup with dried beans, barley, cooked with a smoked bone that gave it a great taste. Nobody kept us more than two or three nights, however, and we didn't want to stay either. We were getting impatient.

More Russian trucks were on the road, and we had more hope of being transported. They stopped and asked us where we were going. We answered Transylvania – Hungary -- Romania. If they were headed south, they picked us up for a couple of miles and we were content.

Chapter Twenty:
Mama ~ Omnipotent

One late afternoon when the sky was dark, it was threatening to snow and it was still very cold. Two trucks reached us near a gas station. The first truck driver looked at me with sympathy and said, "You are frozen, little girl. Come with me in the front of the truck. It's warmer. The rest of you will come in back of the other truck."

I said my mother should come with me. He said there was no room for two people in front, but both trucks were going to the same destination.

Mama pushed me to go. "Warm up. I will go with the other girls in the other truck," she said.

The Blau sisters declared I was a selfish, spoiled brat and should stick with the group. Of course everybody was cold, they said, why should I be privileged just because I was younger or maybe prettier? Yet from our miserable looking clothes, which showed only our faces from our mouths to our foreheads, my face could hardly be seen. Mama didn't care, but just urged me to go and said we were meeting at the train station where both trucks were headed.

The soldiers had no time to waste. My driver followed the truck with his group, and he opened the front door while the girls climbed into the back of the other truck. I could see them, but they didn't look at me. Only Mama waved.

I now realize what a stupid, selfish child I was. This was the first time Mama and I had separated for even a short time. Why did I listen to her? Why was I so weak? She needed the warmth more than I did. I couldn't speak; I just pushed myself into the corner of the seat and tried not to cry.

I could see the truck in front of us until it started to get darker. Our truck slowed down and I lost them. I also noticed that my driver looked at me with curious eyes, and freed his right hand from the steering wheel. He touched me on my left leg above the blanket, and then started to undo the blanket and move his hand between my legs. We were in the middle of a dark forest -- nobody could come to my rescue.

I got really scared and began to cry. I could say one thing: "Mama, help me." I didn't speak Russian, but knew how to say "mat" and "mama," an international word. He stopped the truck completely and moved to my corner. No matter how I pulled, I could not open the truck door.

My tears and my shouting "Mama" awakened him in the middle of his intention to rape me. As if from a dream, suddenly he looked into my eyes in the dark and realized he could not satisfy his animal desires.

He said, "Too bad you are a little girl," and showed with his hands what a baby I was.

All this lasted only a couple of minutes, but seemed like an eternity. I cried silently with relief and also with worry about when I would see my Mama. Just mentioning Mama's name saved my virginity. Who would believe that a Russian soldier, a young man three years into the war, would stop before committing a brutal crime because he realized he was a human being. Maybe he realized he also had a mother and maybe sisters -- and who would protect them?

I thought I would never again see the others and Mama would be heartbroken. My driver was now in a hurry and speeded up. Twenty minutes later we arrived in the station. Mama was waiting desperately alone in the dark waiting room. All the girls had abandoned her because she had such a selfish daughter. I never forgave myself for their cruelty -- to leave my mother in the middle of the night, not even waiting for half an hour for my truck.

Mama was in tears and so concerned that when I hugged and kissed her, she fell into my arms and would not let go for minutes. My truck driver looked at us with emotion, and then showed a guiltless smile on his face. He was very pleased with himself that he could control his instincts. Mama didn't ask anything, didn't talk, just clung to me without words. Finally, we looked around. I saw the other driver sleeping in the corner of the small waiting room. No one else was there. There were no trains or travelers.

We had no idea what to do. We decided to walk in the dark until we saw the light of a house where we could sleep.

The first house was not too far from the station. All the girls were there eating hot potatoes on the kitchen floor. Leon was furious. How could I have done this to my mother? Even so, she offered us two potatoes and half a turnip. She said we would have some coffee soon. The others ignored us. There was an old Polish woman who felt sorry for Mama and gave her a piece of homemade cheese. There was also a fire in the stove and we fell asleep where we were sitting in the kitchen, holding each other and promising never to separate again.

We kept our promise until Mama died on November 5, 1999.

The next day Mama and I and two other girls went on our own toward the center of the village. We had heard from a Jewish man we met on the street that there was a so-called "Jewish Center" which registered strangers which could give us some shelter for a day or two. It was not difficult to find this village. It was a shtetl for lots of Jews, and everybody knew everybody. Now there were about twenty young men and two to three couples without any children or families. These people had come back home from hiding or were liberated by the Russians, just as we were.

The couple who took Mama and me into their home spoke Yiddish, so Mama was their first choice to be invited to stay with them for a couple of days. They were happy to see some survivors, even Hungarian Jews. They showed us to their two horse carriage and it carried us to their house. The other two girls went with a younger man whose parents were expected home any day, so he had free space until they returned. We agreed to meet the girls at the nearest train station in a day or two.

We were in the carriage when the man lifted a rag covering the back, and showed us how much fresh meat he had -- half of a beef, some large sheep legs, and some veal.

"We'll have enough to eat," he said. "This is good business." We listened and didn't ask too much. We just wanted to settle in a room soon.

The couple carried the meat into the adjacent room, and then went to the kitchen to cook a late lunch for us. We had never had a more hearty stew in our lives: all kinds of dry vegetables -- beans, potatoes, barley, lentil, and cabbage -- and smoked beef all in one dish. They even served brown bread and black tea at the end.

I have never forgotten that meal.

As soon as we could say good night, we excused ourselves and went to our room. We didn't know what these people were doing in the kitchen, but two to three hours later, seemingly in the middle of the night, we woke up to a big, loud argument in Polish. The man and the woman were yelling at each other. I couldn't help being curious, and looked through the keyhole. They each had a big knife and hammers in their hands, and were gesticulating, and cutting up the animals which were hanging from the ceiling.

I was terribly frightened. Mama also had to look, and said quietly, "They are butchers."

I was afraid they would kill each other in the heat of their argument, and we would be blamed. We started to timidly knock at the door, pretending to ask for water. They stopped immediately and explained to Mama how hard it was to make a living by selling meat clandestinely, and said they were arguing about to whom they should bring the meat pieces in the middle of the night. They hoped we would not report them to the officials.

Mama reassured them. "We are only miserable people who are grateful to have a bed to sleep in and for the great food you have given us."

These were good, very simple, hardworking people, who were trying to live through the war and start over their interrupted life they enjoyed until 1939.

Chapter Twenty One:
Treblinka Train Station

Treblinka was an unforgettable stop on our long journey home. We walked the entire day in cold and snow, without hope of finding transportation, and we stopped at this so-called train station that resembled a one-room hut, without a bathroom or toilets. It was mid-afternoon and we had little energy left. Some of the girls hoped we could board a train immediately. We were told the name of the place was Treblinka, and that in three days there would be a train that would go to the border. We were told that we must have patience.

The room was almost full when we settled on the floor -- twelve of us odd-looking Jewish girls, covering our numbers from Auschwitz on our clothes. It was getting darker and there was only one lamp hanging from the ceiling that had about one quart of petroleum feeding the light. We opened our worn out bags and sorted out the food we had. Who knew when we would be able to get more of this bread, butter, and smoked meat we had saved from the last house where we had stopped for a day or two?

We always shared our food. We had one bottle of tea that was hot in the morning and lukewarm by afternoon. We carried it in our bags so it warmed the sides of our bodies. We also had cold baked potatoes from the night before and we ate them along with some raw turnips.

We placed our dishes on the floor of the station with the forks and knives that we had gotten at the first farm after our liberation. Mama began to say a prayer that we all knew, and we could hardly wait for the first bite. There were about forty women in that station, and they watched us with fascination. They spoke Polish and Russian and did not mingle with us. Their meals were no more elaborate than our own: onion, garlic that we could smell, and yellow cornbread like the kind our peasants in Romania used to bake. They had big chunks of bacon that they cut with pocket knives, which they also used as eating utensils. They all looked tired, but they were in much better physical condition than we were, and some of them were even heavy and strong. Even so, we all ate equally slowly so that our food would last longer.

When it was completely dark outside we were ready for the night and tried to sleep sitting close to one another with our backs against the wall and our blankets covering us. If someone had to go to the toilet outside, she had to be careful not to step on anyone and not to hurt anyone.

We tried to leave a small passageway in front of the door, but some of those with longer legs created an obstacle in the dark.

After a while everyone fell asleep. There was no sign of the train coming. Our heads rested on our chests or on each other's shoulders.

In the middle of the night we awoke to a big commotion. Soldiers were coming into the station, singing loudly, their drunken voices rushing at us through the door. In the flickering light of the petroleum lamp their faces looked cruel.

The first three men realized there was no place for them to sit unless they lay upon us, Mama was quick to move onto my lap and covered both of us with her blanket. I almost suffocated -- I could get only a little bit of air under her elbow.

The first man put his feet on the empty place in front of Mama and began shouting, "Barishnya! Barishnya!" (Woman! Woman! Lady! Lady!) And one of his hands reached out toward Mama while the other motioned for his pants. Mama cried out in her desperation and showed her short hair to the man.

She said in Hungarian, "I am a babushka -- an old woman, sick and skinny. Leave me alone." She was crying and pushing the big man away.

The other women were petrified because they heard shouting and shooting outside. About one yard from us a heavy-set woman watched Mama struggle with the drunken soldier who was ready to rape her. The woman laughed at him out loud, crawled towards the man, stood up and pulled him away, still laughing and talking to him in Russian. "Idiot, idiot. Babushka is sick and filthy! Come to me. Let's get out of here!"

Everyone watched the scene except me, because I was covered completely by my struggling mother.

The Russian woman did not give up. She was stronger and knew how to deal with the drunken man. Actually, she seemed to have fun pulling this man off my mother, helping him to his feet, and dragging him out into the cold air. Mama said later she had seen that woman both before and after the attack; she was a happy, conquering, wild animal who had found her mate and expected a great prize at the end of her fight.

That happened outside the waiting room, as Susie told us later, for she had gone to search for a toilet. The other men who had guns shot them into the air until the petrified women they had grabbed succumbed.

For Mama and me, it was an incredible relief that the big Russian woman wanted that man and that she had saved us from this drunken animal. Only then did Mama slowly move off of my lap and I could breathe again. We fell asleep.

What happened at the train station in Treblinka is one of my worst memories.

We waited for two days and two nights until finally, a coal-carrying wagon arrived after having disposed of its cargo. Some men who were black from the coal looked at us and said in Czech, "You won't have a luxurious trip with this train, but go ahead. There is no charge and it goes to the south of the country."

Our Czechoslovakian friends jumped up into the wagon and we followed them. They had understood what the man had said. We only saw the opening of the wagon, the door, but inside the smell and mess was disgusting. Feathers from half-opened pillows filled the wagon like gray snow; remnants of food were everywhere, and there was human excrement in the corners of the wagon but there was no returning to the station. The train moved forward with a big bang and the doors closed as soon as we started down the hill. It was miserable. We could not even sit until we cleaned a spot for our rags using the half-empty pillows that were still wet with urine.

After an hour or so, the train stopped in an open field. It was pitch dark and we did not know what to do. If we opened the doors and got out, we might freeze to death and would have survived for nothing!

"I want to see my father," I yelled in frustration.

We sat in the dark and waited for the train to move on. Perhaps we fell asleep, because when we awoke we saw the morning sunshine through the small window of the wagon and through the now opened door. We did not waste a minute, jumped out onto the platform of a nice, small train station. Treblinka the nightmare was behind us, but would never be forgotten.

Thirty years later, I read a book entitled *Treblinka* that recorded the tragedy of the Jews who staged a rare uprising, but nevertheless had been killed in the forests before the gas chambers were invented. Mama and I recalled our experience.

"God was with us," Mama said.

Chapter Twenty Two:
The Remnants of
Civilization - Warsaw

Since we never had a map, I did not know where we were. Actually, Warsaw was non-existent as a city -- only ruins were in front of us, chimneys, bombed out building bare walls remained. In its outskirts was Praga, Warsaw's suburb where we spent just one day and one night. It was a ghost town.

In 1994, fifty years later, I returned to Auschwitz and also spent a day in Warsaw. It had been completely rebuilt -- exactly as it was before the war, in order to keep the dignity of the Polish capital. I visited Chopin's house and attended a beautiful concert just to detach myself from the painful memories. I went to their Cemetery of Heroes and to the place where the ghetto used to be.

In 1945, Praga was crowded -- overpopulated with people from Warsaw who had lost their homes or business and were trying to find temporary homes. The Poles were bitter and hopeless. They didn't feel sympathy for us Jews. A bank clerk at whose house we were staying, told us that we had never had a homeland and a capital. We were a wandering tribe, nomads, he said, who cried for the Jerusalem of our Bible. We'd better get out of this country soon, he said, and find our fatherland -- or die. After this "advice," we didn't feel like spending one more minute there. We left at five o'clock in the morning while it was still dark, and ran for half an hour until we couldn't catch our breath.

After many days of walking and resting in different villages, we reached the town of Lvov. The first building was a mill where we looked for safety. We entered it and saw mattresses on the floor and flour-whitened wood boards. The air was filled with the smell of fresh wheat which had turned into white powder. We didn't have to wait too long to see a worker bringing in a huge pot of steaming soup. The man was preparing for all the wandering groups of people who spent time there. We got out our old camp dishes and spoons, and found places to sit. He put the pot on a low stool and ladled it into our dishes.

Two handsome men, perhaps twenty-three and twenty-five years old, stepped in, neatly dressed with fur hats and leather boots. One of them spoke German and French, and showed a real interest in our story. We were the first women liberated from the German concentration camps they had seen. These men also had been prisoners in

Polish slave labor camps, and they had escaped and joined the partisans. Later, they joined the Russian army.

In January, the one named Ludwig, a Jew, came home because he had been wounded. He did not find anybody from his family. All their valuables had been looted from his house. His mother and father had been taken to Treblinka and never returned. He had heard that Treblinka was an extermination camp. He and his childhood friend Janos, who was Christian, fought against the Germans together.

They both had started college, but Ludwig, being Jewish, had to stop after one year. Janos continued, but then the war also stopped his studies. He joined the Russian army where he met his friend Ludwig. They had remained together ever since, both having become orphans. In Ludwig's mill Polish people worked as if it were their own property. When the owner's son, a young man, came home, he took over the mill and produced three times as much flour than the usual unskilled workers were able to get from his crop.

I could talk to Ludwig. The other man, Janos, spoke only Polish and some French, which we preferred and avoided German. I liked Ludwig immediately and related to him everything that had happened to us in the ten months since we left Hungary. He was full of sympathy and ready to help all of us. He ordered dinner -- cold cuts, a huge fresh white bread, pickles, and milk, which we hadn't had for a long time. There were some sinks with water in the mill, primitive toilets, but we were not complaining. The two men slept on mattresses just to be with us, or maybe to guard the first surviving women they had encountered.

Ludwig came to us and we spoke for a long time while everybody else was asleep. He hugged us and comforted us with his kind words, and he promised to visit us after the war. He asked us to stay with him as long as we wanted, and if I wanted to stay in Lvov, he said, he would marry me. In my circumstances, that was so wonderful and incredible.

He said that his house had been bombed, but he had an apartment in his neighbor's house -- Christians, who had been friends of his parents. His housekeeper was a baroness, an aristocrat, he said, who cooked and washed for Ludwig. She had saved everything she could from his parents' house and treated him as her own son. This lady was very protective of Ludwig. She invited Janos and me for lunch the next day.

Mama was in very bad condition, she weighed only ninety-three pounds. She wouldn't come with us. Ludwig asked me if I had table manners, if I knew how to use a knife and fork in front of this Baroness. He looked at my clothing and asked if I had anything else to wear. Of course I didn't, I told him. He said that he would bring something that would be presentable. I didn't tell him I still had lice in my dress. I was too ashamed, and asked for a skirt and a sweater to keep me warm when I would take off my blanket-coat.

The next day he brought breakfast to everybody: real butter, a huge white bread, as big as the tire of a car, smoked ham, and a bucket of milk. When we couldn't eat any more, we thanked him many times. Some girls went into the town. Mama and two women wanted to stay and relax in the mill and wash their clothing. I washed my short hair and put on the clothing that Ludwig had brought for me, cleaned my worn out shoes, and started to feel like a human being again.

Ludwig told me to only answer questions without asking anything. Talk as little as possible during the meal with the Baroness. She scrutinized everything about me, so much that I could not enjoy the meal, which was unusual, but very tasty. Finally, during coffee, she started asking questions, and listened to me with incredulous eyes. This was more in French than in German.

At the end, she asked, "How come you survived?"

I said I was lucky that Mama was with me. We had supported each other, and her faith in God never left us. Ludwig said that my greatest success was that the Baroness invited me again the next week. I thanked her, but did not accept, for I did not know where I would be by then.

While we were walking back to the mill, Ludwig pointed out the town's main square- Kosciusko Avenue -- with the statue of this great general. He showed me other landmarks he was so proud of, like the University. Unfortunately, there were only two social classes in Poland, he said. One strives for progress, culture and education.

The other, very low class, was poor, disinterested in the future, and lived from one day to the next. They were mostly illiterate, and therefore angry and bitter. This was why the Poles were so mean and hated everybody who lived better than they did, he said.

This was the only place where I would have stayed longer -- at least four or five days more. Ludwig was so attentive and concerned about how we would continue our trip on roads full of soldiers, runaways, beggars, and thieves. But the other girls didn't want to stay. They were in a hurry, and were restless.

Ludwig heard about a train that was going from Lvov to Lublin the next day, and we could get on it for free. He went to a kind of Jewish community service which gave us papers, individually, that stated that we had been prisoners in Nazi camps and wanted to get back home. I kept this paper until we reached Transylvania and then ripped it into one hundred pieces. It wasn't needed anymore; and it was useless anyway.

Janos, Ludwig's friend, brought us food for the trip, big packages with all kinds of goodies that lasted for four days. It was really hard to say goodbye to Ludwig. We sat in the corner of the small waiting room and I knew that we would never meet again. We exchanged addresses, though, and we talked about our future. I, finishing high school, he finishing college -- we would meet and start a new life.

Ludwig said, "At least we'll have one mother."

He did not believe that his parents would ever return. I can still see him from the train waving goodbye to the departing train, tears flowing down his cheeks, trying to smile. I never received any letters from him, though. They may have been lost, because it was still war when we arrived in Transylvania, and the postal service was minimal. I wrote only one letter to him, in June 1945, but didn't get any answer. I will remember him forever as a great friend and maybe I was even in love with him a little, he was so handsome.

Chapter Twenty Three: Humane - Last Stop Before Romania

April is usually windy and sunny after the cold late-winter rain in Eastern Europe, and in 1945 it was no different. Unfortunately, the three months hardship of our journey in the bitter cold had badly affected Mama's health, and my own health suffered, too. I had a fever every day and became so weak that we had to stop for days in April to recuperate before we could continue on our way.

In a refugee hospital where many women were already resting, I got minimal and primitive help. Mama and I were accepted there, as war victims, liberated prisoners, and concentration camp slave-laborers who were trying to go on with their lives. There were clean mattresses for thirty women in a huge hall that was heated by ovens. The volunteer nurses treated us with kindness, but they had little medication. Hot compresses, aspirin, and warm soups helped us rest. The two Blau sisters and Leon needed treatment too, and joined us there. We were the first Hungarian Jewish former prisoners from the same camp to go home.

When the head nurse asked Mama and me the name of our hometown, she had surprisingly happy news for us. She said that a doctor who had survived Auschwitz after being in a slave labor camp in the Ukraine, had met his wife who had worked in an Auschwitz hospital, there at the hospital in Humane a week ago. They were headed to Kolozsvar (Cluj) also. It was a unique event and the two were the happiest couple on earth, she said. They were Uncle Miki and Luisa, Mama's second cousins! We were overjoyed and gained hope that some of our family, at least the young people, would come home. We wanted to hasten our recovery and to heading home with the last bit of our strength. We were all energized by the news, but unfortunately our legs did not obey our wishes.

My fever was stubborn and the only doctor who saw me discouraged me from leaving, and expressed concern about my heart condition. As it turned out, he correctly diagnosed tonsillitis, pneumonia, and early rheumatism.

In my senior year of high school, one year later, I had pneumonia again, and Uncle Miki cured it with vitamins. Dr. Weinstein removed my tonsils the same year. In the last ten years, I have suffered from serious osteoarthritis, which was first diagnosed as juvenile arthritis, beginning in my teenage years. Sleeping on the floor for eleven months had crippled my joints and bones.

We waited for only a couple of days when we found out that there was a train that would take us from Humane across the border into Romania, to Nagy-Karoly, in former Hungary. No one could hold us back any longer. We grabbed our backpacks and some food. I threw away my last piece of camp clothing (which was still infested with lice). I could not stand it anymore. Had I saved it, it would have been given to the Holocaust museum in New York or Washington. I received a wool dress from one of the volunteers who had pity on me, and we left that hospital which was filled with kind, gentle, and loving people.

Although the war was not over yet, many people filled the trains who were mostly homeless prisoners and liberated camp survivors. It was the most civilized transportation we had experienced so far, and some people even managed to get seats on the wooden benches. There were windows that opened and people offered water or hot tea to those who needed it. We were the most miserable looking lot of the passengers.

We had been reunited with the Klein sisters from our hometown. They had been liberated from the same camp, although we had lost each other on our journey. We were all very skinny, pale, horribly dressed (still using blankets as coats), and our short hair was filthy.

We arrived in Nagy-Karoly in the daytime, and many people watched as our train arrived because it was the first one to come from other countries. A pharmacist who was expecting his young wife, Friss Magda (who was a friend from my home town) to return any day and came every day to the station in the hopes of seeing her, was at the station. When the seven of us got off, he ran to us. Mama and I had news for him. We had seen his wife in Stutthof, and we thought she might still be alive. He was so happy and hopeful, he took us all to his home. He had not been deported, but had been sent to a forced slave labor camp in the country. He had been free in Romania since January and reopened his pharmacy and decorated his home for his wife. We gave him hope for awhile, but unfortunately, his wife never came back.

That day he treated us like queens, however. He asked what we craved for most. Mama said a bath, I said an apple, and the Blau girls asked for a real bed. Leon wanted to eat a cake and read the newspaper, and the Klein sisters wished for plum brandy. We all got what we wanted and much more. We stayed two or three days, but we wanted to get home because we still had a long way to go. There was no regular transportation, so we hired coaches with money the pharmacist had given us. He had "lei," Romanian money that we had not seen since 1939.

The coach took us to our next stop, Nagy-falu, where the Klein sisters had a cousin who was already home. (This Klein is still alive and lives in Forest Hills, New York.) He drove the seven of us home to Cehul-Silvaniei (no longer known by its Hungarian name "Szilagy-Cseh"), in a horse drawn carriage.

We were the first women to come back to our town after surviving the Holocaust.

After May 8th, when the war was officially over, five more women returned to our town and one, who was married, found her husband at home. There were also some men who were not deported, and had survived the Hungarian forced labor camps.

Mr. Klein informed us of the number and names of Jews who had returned to our town; at that point there had been about twenty-five altogether, but none from our family. We were not surprised that six hundred people from our town were still missing but we planned to prepare everything for their homecoming after the war. We had much to do, and would try our best to offer, besides our love, some comfort.

Chapter Twenty Four: Friends At Home

It was the end of April -- a Thursday, though I do not know the exact date, when we stepped down from the two-horse coach into the middle of the village at the fountain that was fifty yards from my house. This fountain provided the drinking water for the town's entire population. Those who lived far from it carried the water in buckets and big pitchers. People used the rainwater that was stored in big barrels only for washing bedding and clothes.

I have never tasted better water in my life than that of the fountain at Szilagy-Cseh.

The news of our arrival preceded us, and a lot of people, onlookers and neighbors, were gathered at the entrance to our house. They hugged and kissed us as though we had only returned from a long trip. Even those who had been there and seen us depart on May 3rd under the heavy burden of our backpacks -- those who had hidden behind closed windows and lowered curtains and shades and ignored our pleas for water, even when they came to see us.

They told us how sorry they were for us all this time. No one asked anything of us, our appearances reflected the suffering of our long journeys. My mother's good friend, Tercsike, was the first to bring us food, baskets of apples and grapes. She cried looking at us, and noted how skinny Mama was and how pale I looked. (She was still a robust woman to say the least, at two hundred pounds and only four and a half feet tall!)

But when we entered our empty house, our hearts almost stopped beating. Everything had been taken except the heavy carved wood dining room set, our piano, and two beds. These pieces had been too heavy to carry out, and there must have been no more room in the truck that took our belongings away. We sat on the bed motionless until our tears started to flow. Now we realized that what we missed most were not our things, but our *home* and the warmth of our comfortable, simply decorated house.

Our friends made sure that we had food for two or three days, and they made a fire in the stove. The looters had not completely emptied our log cabin that was ten yards from the kitchen. That is where I later found some pictures of my family and old documents, such as my parents' marriage certificate, our school certificates, and love letters from Ervin dated 1943 and 1944. I could not bring these papers to France or to the United States in 1962 because Communist Party rules forbade the removal of any handwritten papers or books. Then our friends left us and we remained there, but could not sleep.

In the room behind the store where my father had manufactured shoes, we found some pillows and blankets left by the last occupants, soldiers who had lived there for three months. Our neighbors brought some pillowcases and quilts so that we could sleep comfortably in our sweet home. It was a painful night. The past haunted us; the present seemed hopeless, and the future was unknown. How could we start a new life without our family? What kind of work would we find to make a living? We were not beggars anymore, and we could not accept charity.

Neither my mother nor I could fall asleep. We lay silent for hours choosing not to speak because we were afraid of each other's worry.

Early in the morning, my friend Ildiko knocked at the door. She was the pharmacist's daughter who lived across the street. She was older than I, but we had gone to school together until 1940 and continued to play together until we were forbidden to meet, and I was sent to a Jewish school. We looked at each other and she cried and embraced me.

She pointed to a dress that she had folded over her arm. "I knew you would come home. Here is your sweet sixteen dress." It was navy velvet and had a lace collar. "I saved it from the truck that carried away all your stuff. I put it among my dresses so no one would know that it belonged to a Jewish girl."

It was punishable to hide Jewish goods.

How tragic and comical it was to have my velvet dress and no other clothing to change into. Ildiko's action had a more profound message for me, though: it was the sign of true friendship regardless of the difference in our religions. This gave me the faith to believe that not everybody hated us. She took a risk to make me feel cared for, and she expected me to return to life as it was before the Nazis.

I looked at her honest face. She was smiling and crying with joy to have me back. She had all kinds of plans for me: she would lend me a tennis racket, books that she had read in the last year, notes from her junior year of high school, everything that she could to help me with my schooling and well-being. For me this was the first light I had seen at the end of our dark tunnel.

The next day another very important proof of friendship helped to revive my crushed identity. Joseph, who had been the son of my father's former employee, and also my age, came to see us carrying a big box in his arms. We had to open the door for him because he did not have a free hand to reach the handle.

I looked at his big brown eyes, shiny with tears, and put my hands on the box to help him lower it to the floor. He hugged me, embarrassed as he did so because, after all, he was an eighteen-year old boy, and I was a maturing girl. He asked us to excuse his parents who were working and would come by to see us when they were done.

To cover his excitement, he bent down close to the box and opened it. It was my accordion! I learned to play it because I was not a very good pianist. Even though my brother, Zoltán, did not think much of it as a musical instrument, I had loved it!

I jumped up and down with joy to see this dear friend who brought me my treasure. He had picked up the accordion on the street when the soldiers emptied our house. The box was in shambles because Joe had to hide it in the ground for three months until the soldiers left our village. The accordion was in great condition, though, and I still had it in 1962 when we left Romania. Before we left, I gave it to Joseph's son.

Joe said that his father had saved my father's winter coat, and that he would bring it that afternoon. This meant so much to us. Mama and I could believe in friendship again in spite of the hatred that the Nazis and Hungarian fascists inflicted on our village's population. We did not think anymore that all our Christian friends forgot us and had cooperated with the Nazis to annihilate us.

It was the end of April and the war was still going on. During our imprisonment in the camps we thought the world had stopped because no one had lifted a finger to help us; it seemed that everyone had accepted Hitler's domination. In Riga, when we saw the "Stalin candles," we thought that only the Russians were fighting back, but that was in August of 1944. Since that time, only the sounds of cannons in Guttau had given us some hope that Hitler might be defeated and the war would end.

On January 21th when the Russians liberated us, we realized that we were no longer prisoners, but also that there was no peace in Europe. Now, the Russians were still pushing the enemy out of their homeland and the Germans refused to realize the fact that they would not be conquering the world. Their retreat was dangerous because they would shoot unexpectedly from hidden places, such as empty houses, and burn everything behind them.

We still had not read any newspapers or listened to the radio. We did not know that in June 1944 the Allies had landed in Normandy and liberated the countries of Western Europe that the Nazis had conquered and whose populations they had subjugated. These nations had their economies, cultures, and history destroyed in the name of "Deutschland, Deutschland Über alles" (Germany, Germany above all).

We were home now but not in Hungary -- in Romania. Hungary, which had been cooperating with the Germans, had lost Transylvania again, just as they had after World War I. That was comforting to us, because the Hungarian government had been horrible to the Jews and, after they deported us, the Romanians of Transylvania became second class citizens as well.

There were no Romanian schools and the administration was completely Hungarian. The best jobs in business were given to Hungarians, and the remaining odd jobs were left to Romanians. Hungarians owned land while the Romanians were the small farmers and peasants. We were informed of this by both ends of the community, but Szilagy-Cseh was mostly Hungarian and, of course, they did not admit their oppression of the Romanians.

Our friends from other small villages and past customers told us how they lived under Hungarian occupation. Conditions had become worse over the previous year as Hitler came to consider only the Hungarians to be his last trustworthy allies.

A Romanian farmer brought us a radio. He was the man who had wanted to hide me. My father was willing to accept his offer but I did not want to be separated from my family. We began listening to the news, and, as we did, we knew that the war would soon be over. Of course, we hoped that the end of the war would bring my father, brother, strong uncles, aunts, and cousins home to be reunited. But until then I would have to find work to make a living for us, because my mother would be busy trying to recreate our home with Uncle Gyula's family, and Grandmother Luisa, and would have to prepare the other homes of her four brothers and their families' homecoming.

We had so much to do that I could not think of the fever I still suffered from daily, or my mother's swollen ankles, or her lost teeth. They would be taken care of when the war ended and we could "live" again.

On May 8, 1945 the Germans were officially defeated and World War II ended. The radio was blasting the news and the whole village was celebrating. I was already working as a clerk in the village hall, thanks to a former classmate a Romanian boy. He knew me in the fourth grade and remembered me as the number one student.

He was only eighteen years old, but had become the main clerk in the budgeting department of the village. I earned very little money, but I received coupons for flour, soap, and petroleum for lamps (we had no electricity in our village.) This was a great help, because everything had been rationed during the war and the three years that followed.

I started to study at night to recover my sophomore year that was interrupted in March of 1944. Petroleum was an expensive commodity, and I had to study every night by the light of the lamp in order to take the exams in July and August, so I would be prepared for my senior year in September.

I had the will, but I did not know how to succeed in my plans. Every day was an achievement, and we hoped it would bring us closer to the arrival of our dear ones. I had two new dresses made by our former dressmaker, one for work and one for occasions to come.

At the end of May three more former prisoners arrived. They were men who had been in Auschwitz with my father and Zoltán. One of them, Moshe Markowitz, approached me one day on the street and told me the story of my brother and as much as he knew of my father. He did not have the courage to face me when he first arrived, even though he knew I was home.

The first day after my father and Zoltán had been selected for road construction work, an SS stopped in front of my brother who was chopping stone slowly, taking care not to injure his fingers. He yelled the usual, "Los, los arbeiten!" ("Work!").

My brother showed him his long fingers and told him that he was a piano player and the work would ruin his career. The next moment the soldier pulled his gun laughingly, and shot my brother in front of my father. He then walked away, cursing Jews for their fancy occupations.

Moshe and another man carried Zoltán away from the construction site to the nearest barracks where other dead bodies lay. My father had to continue to work without uttering a sound of his pain and misery at the death of his only son. Moshe saw my father in the next two to three months in Auschwitz, but then he was sent to another workplace. He had heard that my father and others were evacuated from Auschwitz when the Russians were close and that he was in the Death March. Moshe named the men who had marched with my father, but he did not know his fate. I still had hope that he was alive.

Years passed, but I still had hope. One day, Fishu, my brother's friend, came home and told me that he had been a prisoner with his father and mine. They had both survived the Death March, but they were so weak that after a couple of days before May 8th, first his father, and then my father, had died in a prison camp.

About this time my cousin Irene came home with her stepmother, and soon after they left for Israel. She said she could not live in the village from which her father had been taken away, deported, and killed in a gas chamber.

The days, weeks, and months passed. No good news came of our family. Thirty-seven members of our family were missing. Mama and I still had hope and turned a deaf ear to the terrible stories of the gas chambers, Nazis murdering children and torturing old people. We could not, and did not talk about it freely until we were in the United States. It was too painful and no one would listen to or believe our words. But I knew deep in my heart that the time would come when I would speak up as I had promised my dying camp mates -- that I would tell the world the truth and make it my mission as long as I lived, so that it will never happen again.

My mother Pepi and I believed that the next generation of our people and the next after that, are here to stay and that all the people in the world should live and love, and work for a better, just, and free society.

Epilogue

Our life after 1945 had been determined by a strong desire to fulfill the dreams of my father, my family, and my friends who were annihilated before they could reach their dreams. We, the survivors, had to prove to ourselves that we were able to create a better world, and that we could inspire the new generation with compassion for life for everybody.

We were the first nine women to arrive at the end of 1945. Mama and I lived in our almost empty house until neighbors brought some furniture, bedding, photos, and pans that they saved from the Nazi looters. A former classmate who worked in the town hall helped find me a job as a filing clerk. This helped us live because I was given food coupons that were used for flour, sugar, soap, and petroleum for our lamps. This allowed me to study at night after work and to complete my unfinished sophomore year of high school. In three months time I completed my junior year exams. By the end of August I was ready for the twelfth grade that I had to attend at a public school in Cluj.

It was not easy to refuse the single men who found themselves alone without any family and were eager to get married. I had to tell them that my father's legacy was his intention that I should finish my schooling, including college, and then marry.

In 1950 I took the state examination at Victor Babes University -- it was the equivalent of a Master's degree, plus mandatory courses in communist ideology. I worked all my student years to support myself. Mama tried to work in business because she could not continue my father's shoe manufacturing. All the equipment was gone. My father's two brothers and sisters helped us somewhat, but after 1946, the communist regime forbade any correspondence or help from capitalist countries.

In 1947, my freshman year at the university, I met a wonderful man, Paul, who was studying to be a pharmacist and had lost all his family in the Holocaust. He became my husband in 1950 when we both fulfilled our parents' dreams and became college graduates. From our marriage came our everlasting "raison de vivre," our son, born in 1955. He carries in his genes and in his spirit the duty to tell his children, Rachel and Robert, that our family is here to stay and should never forget our people.

For a short period legal appeal was given to the population -- mainly Jews who lost their families -- to emigrate to Israel or to a country where they had relatives and could hope to establish family ties. We were all eager to leave the country where we had suffered so much.

Unfortunately, it was not until 1962 that we could emigrate to France where my mother had a cousin who had survived the Nazi occupation. His sons sent an affidavit for all of us. We were allowed to bring only one piece of luggage each containing only clothes and bedding. We were allowed no valuables and no money. On January 2, 1962 we left our house with furniture, paintings, books and rugs. We could not even take our college diplomas with us; we sent them through the Israeli embassy to friends and afterwards they forwarded them to us in the United States, where we finally settled.

We did not want to stay in France for good. I wanted to see my aunts, uncles, and cousins in New York so that I could be again with close family. Thanks to John F. Kennedy's immigration law, we learned that we could apply for an American visa. While waiting for our visas in Paris, supported by Jewish organizations, I continued my education. I took evening classes in Western Literature which I paid for by tutoring immigrants in English and Hebrew. My husband could not work because he had no working papers and he assumed responsibility for our son's needs (he was a first grader in a private elementary school). The school was far from our refugee-hotel where we lived in modest conditions. But we enjoyed our freedom to study, learn, speak, and participate in whatever cultural events, such as museums and theater, we could afford.

In June we received our entrance visa to the United States. We cried and laughed. Mama prayed and we all hoped we would reach our final destination after eighteen years of insecurity and hopelessness. We crossed the ocean on a ship called the SS America. When we saw the Statue of Liberty and my uncles and aunts waving from the port of New York, we were safe and full of hope.

Looking back on the first two years in New York I remember the Bronx; the subway to Brooklyn; Colby Academy, my first job teaching French and Latin; my husband's job as a pharmaceutical chemist in New Jersey to which he traveled one hour each way every day; my son's education in his fifth language after Hungarian, Romanian, German, and French; and Mama taking care of all of us in our home. It was not easy, but in spite of all these new challenges we were content and we loved America.

In 1964 I got my certification to teach in public school in the U.S. and I got a job in Eastchester, where I taught full time for twenty-six years, and since 1991, as a substitute teacher. My husband, Paul, passed away in that year. He was killed in an industrial accident: a machine fell on him, and this was a catastrophe I could never get over. My son, George, who finished law school in California, married and has two lovely children, still mourns his father, who was his best friend. My mother, who was my support all my married life, stood by me in happiness and sorrow and never lost her faith. She lived with me until the age of one hundred and one and five months when she passed away in our home.

She instilled in me the compassion and unselfish love that enabled me to care for old and young, whoever needs my help. Also, she gave me the hope to project this not only to my family, but also to my friends, my students, and in all my interactions with other people.

My son in Kolozsvár 1977

My son's college graduation

My son's wedding

My son's family

My retirement

My husband, mother and son at my retirement

Breinigsville, PA USA
14 April 2010
236167BV00001B/1/A